the pitfalls of english

# The Pitfalls of English

## A Guide and Reference

Dmitry Orlov

CLUB
ORLOV
PRESS

The Pitfalls of English:
A Guide and Reference

Cover art: *Brain Loss* by Santalucia Art Inc., used
under Standard License from depositphotos.com

Publication date: December 25, 2015

ISBN-13: 978-1522915560
ISBN-10: 1522915567

Club Orlov Press
http://ClubOrlovPress.blogspot.com
cluborlovpress@gmail.com

# Contents

# Introduction

English is an incredibly handy language. In fact, if you only know one language, but it's English, you'll probably manage to get by somehow. It's almost incomparably easier to learn than Chinese, Arabic or Russian. Even Spanish, which is another incredibly handy language, and also fairly easy to learn, has quite a bit more grammatical machinery to it than English: grammatical gender, inflections and so on.

This is why English is in such widespread use all over the world. If a Chinese, a Russian and an Arab meet and have a conversation, it's a safe bet that they will be speaking English. There are many reasons why it's so easy to learn: English grammar is small and simple; English vocabulary is international, much of it borrowed from Latin, Greek, French and other languages; and a bit of English is easy to pick up simply by paying attention, because it has excellent penetration throughout the world via popular music, movies and the Internet.

So far so good. But there is another side to English which makes it rather unnecessarily complicated. While spoken English is easy, written English is so confusing that kids in English-speaking countries spend several more years just learning how to read and write than kids who grow up speaking much more complicated languages, such as the aforementioned Chinese, Russian and Arabic. About half the kids end up having serious difficulties with learning to read and write English.

All the trouble comes from the fact that most English words are still written pretty much the same way they were when they first entered the language—which was often hundreds of years ago, when they sounded very different. For example, when the English first started using the word "nature," they most likely pronounced it "nah-TOO-reh." Now they pronounce it "NAY-chuh," but they still write it as if it were pronounced "nah-TOO-reh." What this means is that for a great many English words (some 40 percent of them) you have to memorize both how they sound *and* how they are written, separately. And that, as an English person might put it, is "a bit of a bother."

And so there is a lot to memorize. But it doesn't stop there. In addition to lots of obsolete spellings, many English words have more than one meaning. This is quite normal (most languages have such words, called **homonyms**), but in English they are sometimes written differently depending on what they mean! These homonyms are called **heterographs**. If you pick the wrong spelling (which is something people do all the time—writing, "break" instead of "brake" or "wave" instead of "waive") dictionaries are of little help and spellcheckers are of no help at all. This book helps you deal with these bothersome special cases with confidence and ease. Luckily, the number of such words is quite small compared to the number of homographic homonyms—words that are spelled the same regardless of how many different meanings they have.

For example, the word "litter" is written the same whether it refers to

a basket of puppies or kittens,
fallen tree leaves,
a cat's toilet supplies,
scattered trash or
a royal traveling bed.

If "litter" were broken up into, say, "litter," "lytter," "littor," "lyttor" and "littre," respectively, would this make English a better language and the world a better place? No, not really! If each distinct meaning of each word were given its own unique spelling, then written English would go beyond "a bit of a bother," and turn into, as an English person might put it, "a bloody nuisance."

You might think that this would be enough punishment already, but no, apparently not! In addition, English has quite a few words that are *pronounced* differently based on what they mean even though they are written the same way. Luckily, most of these have some regularities, and the list of truly random, particularly irksome ones, which have to be memorized individually, is quite short. These are called **heteronyms**, and this book helps you deal with them too.

Are we done yet? Well, almost, but here is where English gets very strange. It has an entire set of words, some of them quite common, which have two contradictory meanings. When you use these words, you have to be extra careful, because you might accidentally express the exact opposite of what you mean. They are called **contronyms**, and this book helps you

3

handle them as well.

Heterographs, heteronyms and contronyms are the three main categories of English pitfalls, and the purpose of this book is to show you how to avoid all of them.

\* \* \*

So how, you are perhaps wondering by now, did a simple language with a small grammar and a largely international vocabulary develop all these problems? In this author's opinion, it is because the English, for hundreds of years now, have been practicing something they call

**one-upmanship** [wən'ʌpmənʃɪp] *noun*
the technique or practice of gaining a feeling of superiority over another person

Of course, in order to appear well-bred and civilized, the English have had to practice their one-upmanship in gentlemanly or ladylike ways. And what better way to do that than by inadvertently embarrassing each other? This has motivated them to come up with as many ways of embarrassing each other as possible, and what better way to do that than to introduce lots of little pitfalls into their language?

But this problem is not limited to those whose misfortune it is to be English. Wherever English is used, the impact one has on society depends to a large extent on one's ability to use it correctly, and so all of us, English or not, must learn to steer clear of its pitfalls.

If English is your native language, your educational achievements and career prospects are to a very large extent determined by your ability to *spell* and to *sound educated*. It is an unfortunate fact that many perfectly intelligent kids are held back in life due to just a single shortcoming: their inability to spell. If they were being taught in Chinese, or Russian or Arabic, this tiny handicap would make hardly any difference at all. Many more English-speaking kids are diagnosed with dyslexia than Chinese, Russian or Arabic-speaking kids, and this comes down to just one root cause: English spelling.

If English is your second (or third or fourth) language, then the worst compliment you can receive from a native English speaker is "Your English is very good!" This is the hypocritical cry of victory in the game of English language one-upmanship. What it means is that your English is very bad indeed, and that without major improvement you won't make it very far educationally, professionally or in polite society. If your English were, in fact, very good, you could be sure that nobody would ever compliment you on it. This is because virtually all native English speakers are insecure in their knowledge of their native tongue, apprehensive that you might one-up them, and so they keep quiet on the subject—unless they think that they can one-up you.

Whether English is your native language or your second (or third or fourth) language, this book will help you to avoid its many pitfalls and gain the upper hand in the game of one-upmanship. Its first part is as a guide that will show you where the pitfalls are located—what heterographs, heteronyms and contronyms exist—so that you know what to watch out for.

The rest of the book is in the form of a dictionary: whenever you aren't sure of a word's spelling, pronunciation or sense, look it up, and if it happens to be a potential pitfall, this book will show you how to avoid it.

*  *  *

If you want to avoid embarrassment and appear intelligent and well-educated while speaking and writing English, this book is for you.

And if you pride yourself on being intelligent, well-educated and at the peak of your game, you should nevertheless take a peek inside this book. It may pique you to discover just how much you still don't know.

Lastly, if you are, in fact, intelligent and well-educated, and like making puns, then this book is for you as well, because with its help you'll be sure not to miss any opportunities to appear very clever.

# Section I:
# Pronunciation Guide

To show how English words sound, this book uses a simplified form of the International Phonetic Alphabet.

The goal is to indicate just those distinctions that are important for understanding English speech, without getting bogged down in all the tiny details of a particular accent or dialect.

Most of the symbols are just Latin characters and sound just like you'd expect; the exceptions are shown below.

The pronunciation guides in this book reflect standard North American English of news broadcasters, although specifically North American or specifically British usage is indicated where necessary.

Stressed syllables are indicated by an apostrophe-like mark placed in front of the stressed syllable.

## Vowels

ɪ   fish
i   str**ee**t
ʌ   c**u**t
æ   c**a**t
a   p**a**sta
ɛ   p**e**t
ɔ   sp**o**t
ʊ   b**oo**k
u   p**oo**l

## Diphthongs

aɪ   k**i**te
aʊ   pr**ou**d
eɪ   M**ay**
oʊ   st**o**ve
ɔɪ   b**oy**

## Consonants

ʃ   **sh**ip
tʃ   **ch**air
ʒ   bei**g**e
dʒ   **j**am
θ   **th**ing
ð   **th**is
j   **y**es
ŋ   si**ng**, so**ng**

## Schwa

ə   c**o**ntrol
(An indistinct, unstressed
  vowel.)

## R-colored Schwa

ɚ   p**er**fect
(Its sound varies a lot
  between accents and
  dialects.)

# Section II:
# Heterographs

**Heterographs** are words that sound the same but are written differently. A more precise name for them is **heterographic homonyms**—same-sounding, differently written.

This section contains all the English words that sound the same no matter how carefully you try pronounce them: there is simply no way to tell them apart based on how they sound. (Of course, it is possible to confuse many more words by pronouncing them sloppily or with a thick accent.)

This section contains a summary of homonyms; how each one sounds and the meanings of each different spelling are detailed in the reference section at the back of this book.

ad, add

adds, ads, adze

ade, aid, aide

aerie, airy

affect, effect

air, e'er, ere, err, heir

aisle, isle

all, awl

allowed, aloud

altar, alter

ant, aunt

ante, auntie

arc, ark

ascent, assent

ate, eight

auger, augur

aught, ought

aural, oral

auto, Otto

away, aweigh

awed, odd

aweful, awful

axel, axle

aye, eye

bail, bale

bailed, baled

bailey, bailie

bailing, baling

bait, bate

baited, bated

baiting, bating

bald, balled, bawled

ball, bawl

band, banned

bard, barred

bare, bear

bark, barque

Barry, berry

base, bass

based, baste

bases, basses

bask, basque, Basque

bat, batt

baud, bawd, bod

bay, bey

bays, beize, beys

beach, beech

beat, beet

beau, bow

beaut, butte

beer, bier

Bel, bel, bell, belle

berth, birth

besot, besought

better, bettor

bight, bite, byte

billed, build

bit, bitt

blew, blue

bloc, block

blond, blonde

boar, Boer, boor, bore

board, bored

boarder, border

bocks, box

bode, bowed

bold, bowled

bolder, boulder

bole, boll, bowl

boos, booze

born, borne, bourn

borough, burrow

bough, bow

boy, buoy

braid, brayed

braise, brays, braze

brake, break

breach, breech

bread, bred

brewed, brood

brews, bruise

bridal, bridle

broach, brooch

brows, browse

bundt, bunt

burger, burgher

bus, buss

bussed, bust

buy, by, bye

buyer, byre

cache, cash

cached, cashed

calendar, calender

call, caul, col

caller, choler, collar

can, Cannes

cannon, canon
can't, cant
canter, cantor
canvas, canvass
capital, capitol
carat, karat
cast, caste
caster, castor
cause, caws
cay, key, quay
cedar, seeder
cede, seed
ceding, seeding
ceiling, sealing
cellar, seller
cell, sell
censer, censor, sensor
cent, scent, sent
cents, scents
cereal, serial
cere, sear, seer, sere
Ceres, series
cession, session
chalk, chock
chard, charred
chased, chaste
cheap, cheep
check, Czech
Chile, chili, chilly
choir, quire
choral, coral
chorale, corral

chord, cord, cored
chute, shoot
cited, sighted, sited
cite, sight, site
cites, sights, sites
clack, claque
clause, claws, Klaus
clew, clue
click, clique
climb, clime
coal, cole
coaled, cold
coarse, course
coat, cote
coax, cokes
cocks, cox, Cox
coddling, codling
coffer, cougher
coin, quoin
colonel, kernel
complement,
   compliment
conch, conk
coo, coup
copped, Copt
cops, copse
core, corps
council, counsel
craft, kraft
crater, krater
creak, creek
crewed, crude

crews, cruise
croc, crock
C, sea, see
cue, Kew, queue
curser, cursor
cygnet, signet
dam, damn
dammed, damned
days, daze
dear, deer
desert, dessert
dew, due
dews, dues
Di, die, dye
died, dyed
dies, dyes
dine, dyne
tach, tack
dire, dyer
discreet, discrete
divers, diverse
doc, dock
do, doe, dough
does, dos, dose,
   doughs, doze
done, dun
draft, draught
dyeing, dying
earn, urn
elude, illude
eunuchs, UNIX
ewes, use, yews

14

ewe, yew, you
eyelet, islet
fain, feign
faint, feint
fair, fare
fairing, faring
fairy, ferry
faker, fakir
farrow, pharaoh
faux, foe
fay, Faye, fey
fays, faze, phase
feat, feet
few, phew
file, phial
fill, Phil
filter, philter
find, fined
finish, Finnish
fir, fur, furr
fisher, fissure
flair, flare
flea, flee
flecks, flex
flew, flu, flue
flocks, phlox
Flo, floe, flow
flour, flower
forego, forgo
foreword, forward
for, fore, four
fort, forte

forth, fourth
foul, fowl
frees, freeze, frieze
friar, fryer
gaff, gaffe
gait, gate
gall, Gaul
gays, gaze
genes, jeans
gild, gilled, guild
gilt, guilt
gnawed, nod.
gneiss, nice
gored, gourd
gorilla, guerrilla
grade, grayed
graft, graphed
grate, great
grays, graze
grease, Greece
greave, grieve
greaves, grieves
grill, grille
groan, grown
guise, guys
gym, Jim
hail, hale
hair, hare
halve, have
halves, haves
hangar, hanger
hart, heart

haut, oh, owe
hay, hey
hays, haze
heard, herd
hear, here
he'll, heal, heel
heroin, heroine
hew, hue, Hugh
hide, hied
higher, hire
liquor, licker
hi, high
hoard, horde, whored
hoarse, horse
hoar, whore
hoes, hose
ho, hoe
hold, holed
hole, whole
holey, holy, wholly
hour, our
hours, ours
humerus, humorous
inc., ink
inns, ins
it's, its
jam, jamb
jewel, joule
knap, nap
knead, need
knew, new
knickers, nickers

| | | |
|---|---|---|
| knight, night | load, lode, lowed | miner, minor |
| knit, nit | loan, lone | minks, minx |
| knits, nits | loath, loathe | missed, mist |
| knob, nob | loch, lock | moan, mown |
| knock, nock | lochs, locks, lox | moat, mote |
| knot, naught, nought | lo, low | mode, mowed |
| know, no, Noh | loon, lune | moire, moray |
| knows, noes, nose | loop, loupe | mood, mooed |
| lacks, lax | loos, lose | moor, Moor, more |
| lain, lane | loot, lute | moose, mousse |
| lama, llama | Lot, lot, lot | morning, mourning |
| lam, lamb | Lot's, lots, lots | morn, mourn |
| lay, lei | lumbar, lumber | mustard, mustered |
| lays, laze, leis | made, maid | nay, neigh |
| leach, leech | mail, male | neap, neep |
| lead, led | main, mane | none, nun |
| leak, leek | maize, Mays, maze | oar, or, ore |
| lea, lee, li | mall, maul, moll | one's, ones |
| lean, lean, lien | manner, manor | one, won |
| leased, least | mantel, mantle | oohs, ooze |
| leas, lees | marc, mark, marque | ordinance, ordnance |
| lessen, lesson | marry, merry | O's, owes |
| liar, lyre | marshal, martial | paced, paste |
| lichen, liken | mask, masque | packed, pact |
| licker, liquor | massed, mast | pail, pale |
| lie, lye | mean, mean, mien | pain, pane |
| lieu, loo, Lou | meat, meet, mete | pair, pare, pear |
| lightening, lightning | men's, mens | pallet, pallette |
| limb, limn | mewl, mule | pall, Paul, pawl |
| limbs, limns | mews, muse | passed, past |
| links, lynx | might, mite | pause, paws |
| literal, littoral | mind, mined | peace, piece |

| | | |
|---|---|---|
| peak, peek, pique | racket, racquet | rote, wrote |
| pealed, peeled | rack, wrack | rot, wrought |
| peal, peel | rain, reign, rein | rough, ruff |
| pea, pee | raise, rays, raze | rout, rout, route |
| pearl, Perl, purl | rapped, rapt, wrapped | roux, rue |
| peer, pier | rap, wrap | rye, wry |
| pencil, pensile | ray, re | sachet, sashay |
| per, purr | reading, reeding | sacks, sax |
| picnick, pyknic | read, red | sailer, sailor |
| pieced, piste | read, rede, reed | sail, sale |
| pincher, pinscher | reads, reeds | saner, seiner |
| pi, pie | recede, reseed | sane, seine |
| place, plaice | reck, wreck | saver, savor |
| plait, plate | reek, wreak | sawed, sod |
| plain, plane | retch, wretch | scald, skald |
| planar, planer | review, revue | scarf, scarph |
| pleas, please | rheum, room | scene, seen |
| pleural, plural | rheumy, roomie, roomy | scull, skull |
| plum, plumb | rho, roe, row | seal, seel |
| polar, poler | rhumb, rum | seamen, semen |
| poled, polled | rhyme, rime | seam, seem |
| Pole, pole, poll | rigger, rigor | seams, seems |
| pone, pony | right, rite, wright, write | seas, sees, seize |
| pore, pour | ring, wring | seek, Sikh |
| praise, prays, preys | rise, ryes | seeks, Sikhs |
| pray, prey | road, rode, rowed | serf, surf |
| pride, pried | roam, Rome | serge, surge |
| pries, prize | role, roll | sewer, sower |
| profit, prophet | rood, rude, rued | sewer, suer |
| pros, prose | roomer, rumor | sew, sol, sow |
| psi, sigh, xi | root, route | shake, sheik |
| quarts, quartz | rose, rows | shear, sheer |

17

shears, sheers
shoe, shoo
shoes, shoos
sic, sick
sics, six
side, sighed
sighs, size
sign, sine
sink, synch
Sioux, sou, sough, sue
skin, soar, sore
slay, sleigh
sleight, slight
slew, slough, slue
sloe, slow
soared, sword
sole, soul
some, sum
sonny, sunny
son, sun
spade, spayed
spoor, spore
staid, stayed
stair, stare
stake, steak
stanch, staunch
stationary, stationery
steal, steel
step, steppe
stile, style
stoop, stoup
storey, story

straight, strait
succor, sucker
suede, swayed
suite, sweet
summary, summery
sundae, Sunday
tacks, tax
tail, tale
tall, tole, toll
taper, tapir
tare, tear
taught, taut
teaming, teeming
team, teem
tear, tier
teas, tease, tees
tea, tee, ti
tenner, tenor
tern, terne, turn
Thai, tie
their, there, they're
threw, through
throes, throws
throe, throw
throne, thrown
thyme, time
ticks, tics
tic, tick
tide, tied
tier, tire
tighten, titan
til, till

timber, timbre
toad, toed, towed
tocsins, toxins
tocsin, toxin
toe, tow
told, tolled
tongue, tung
ton, tonne, tun
tort, torte
to, too, two
tough, tuff
tracked, tract
tray, trey
troopers, troupers
trooper, trouper
troop, troupe
trussed, trust
vain, vane, vein
vale, veil
vary, very
verses, versus
vial, vile, viol
vice, vise
wax, whacks
wade, weighed
wails, Wales, wales,
  whales
wail, wale, whale
wain, wane, Wayne
waisted, wasted
waist, waste
wait, weight
waiver, waver

waive, wave
walks, woks
walk, wok
want, wont
ware, wear, where
warn, worn
war, wore
wary, wherry
way, weigh, whey
weak, week
weald, wheeled,
    wield
weal, wheel
weather, wether,
    whether

weld, welled
wen, when
we're, weir
were, whir
wet, whet
we've, weave
Whig, wig
whiled, wild
while, wile
whined, wind, wined
whine, wine
whirled, world
whirred, word
whither, wither

whit, wit
whoa, woe
who's, whose
why, wye, Wye
worst, wurst
yack, yak
y'all, yawl
yokes, yolks
yoke, yolk
yore, your
you'll, yule

# Section III:
# Heteronyms

**Heteronyms** are words that are spelled the same but sound different depending on what they mean. A more precise name for them is **heterophonic homographs**—different-sounding, written the same.

This section contains all the English words that sound different depending on what they mean: there is simply no way to tell how they should sound by looking at them in isolation. What follows is just a summary of them. The reference section at the end of the book shows how each of these words sounds based on what it means.

| | | |
|---|---|---|
| abstract | desert | permit |
| abuse | detail | pone |
| address | discharge | present |
| advocate | discount | produce |
| affect | dispute | project |
| ally | do | putting |
| appropriate | does | re |
| articulate | dos | read |
| associate | dove | recall |
| attribute | elaborate | record |
| bass | entrance | refuse |
| bow | estimate | reject |
| chamois | evening | resign |
| close | fillet | resume |
| combine | graduate | row |
| complex | house | second |
| compound | increase | separate |
| concrete | insert | sewer |
| conduct | inside | slough |
| construct | intimate | subject |
| consult | invalid | survey |
| content | lead | suspect |
| contest | leading | tear |
| contract | live | transform |
| contrast | minute | transport |
| converse | moderate | use |
| convert | mouth | warehouse |
| convict | nearby | wicked |
| decrease | number | wind |
| defect | object | wound |
| defense | outside | |
| degenerate | overnight | |
| deliberate | peaked | |

# Section IV:
# Contronyms

**Contronyms** are words that have contradictory meanings. This section contains the words which, depending on how they are used, can mean the exact opposite of what you'd expect, tripping you up in unexpected ways. For each of these words, a clue as to their contradictory meanings is given using two words or phrases separated by a slash.

adumbrate: disclose/obscure
against: towards/opposing
anarchic: chaotic/self-organized
apology: excuse/defense
aught: all/nothing
awesome: terrible/wonderful
awful: inspiring/revolting
before: in the past/in front of
bill: payment/invoice
blunt: dull/pointed
bolt: secure/flee
boned: with/without bones
bound: moving/restrained
bred: mated/made by mating
buckle: secure/collapse
certain: undefined/definite
check: payment/bill
cleave: adhere/separate
clip: fasten/detach
constrain: force/contain
consult: give/take advice
contingent: certain/uncertain
continue: resume/postpone
cored: with/without a core
critical: essential/disapproving
custom: common/special
dike: wall/ditch
discursive: directed/ directionless
disposed: available/discarded
dollop: large/small amount
downhill: better/worse
dust: add/remove dust
dusted: with/without dust
effect: result/to cause
either: one of/both
endure: undergo/abide

enjoin: impose/prohibit
execute: initiate/terminate
fast: quick/unmoving
fine: excellent/passable
finished: complete/destroyed
fix: repair/castrate
flog: promote/criticize
forge: strengthen/counterfeit
garnish: provide/deprive
generally: sometimes/always
give out: provide/run out
go: pass/fail
grade: slope/level
handicap: advantage/
  disadvantage
help: assist/prevent
hew: split/join
hold up: support/impede
incomparable: matchless/
  mismatched
lease: provide/receive
left: remained/departed
liege: lord/vassal
literally: actually/virtually
lurid: pale/glowing
mean: average/excellent
model: genuine/replica
moot: debatable/irrelevant
natty: fashionable/bedraggled
off: activated/deactivated
original: old/new
out: visible/invisible
out of: outside/inside
overlook: examine/ignore
oversee: control/disregard
oversight: monitoring/failing

**peer**: nobility/one's equal
**periodic**: regular/irregular
**peruse**: pore over/glance at
**presently**: now/soon
**public**: social/official
**put out**: extinguish/generate
**qualify**: restrict/allow
**quantum**: huge/tiny
**quiddity**: essense/trifle
**quite**: somewhat/entirely
**ravel**: entangle/disentangle
**refrain**: desist/repeat
**rent**: provide/occupy
**reservation**: confirmation/
  uncertainty
**riot**: violent/funny
**sanction**: approve/penalize
**sanguine**: cheerful/bloodthirsty
**scan**: analyze/skim
**screen**: present/conceal
**secrete**: produce/hide
**seed**: add/remove seeds
**several**: single/multiple
**shelled**: with/without shell
**show-stopper**: admirable/
  intolerable

**skin**: cover/strip
**smell**: sniff/stink
**splice**: join/split
**strike**: hit/miss
**suspicious**: distrustful/
  untrustworthy
**table**: advance/withdraw
**temper**: soften/strengthen
**terrific**: wonderful/terrible
**throw out**: offer/discard
**too**: also/excessively
**transparent**: visible/invisible
**trim**: add/remove
**unbending**: stiff/relaxed
**utopian**: perfect/unrealistic
**vain**: proud/futile
**variety**: distinct type/assortment
**vary**: to differ/to change
**want**: desire/lack
**wear**: endure/succumb
**weather**: withstand/deteriorate
**wicked**: evil/good
**wind up**: end/start
**with**: together/against

# Section V:
# Reference

Below are assembled all the **heterographs,** **heteronyms** and **contronyms** of English, in alphabetical order, with pronunciation guides. Use it as you would a dictionary, to look up the different spellings, different pronunciations, and contradictory meanings of English words.

# A

abstract: [ˈæbstrækt] *noun*,
[əbstˈrækt] *adj.*
abuse: [əbjˈus] *noun*,
[əbjˈuz] *verb*
ad [ˈæd]: advertisement
add: to perform addition
add [ˈæd]: to perform addition
ad: advertisement
address: [ˈædrəs] *noun*,
[əˈdrɛs] *verb*
adds [ˈædz]: performs
addition
ads: advertisements
adze: axe
ade [ˈeɪd]: beverage
aid: to help
aide: assistant
ads [ˈædz]: advertisements
adds: performs addition
adze: axe
adumbrate [ˈædəmbreɪt]:
disclose/obscure
advocate: [ˈædvoʊkeɪt] *verb*,
[ˈædvəkət] *noun*

adze [ˈædz]: axe
adds: performs addition
ads: advertisements
aerie [ˈɛɚi]: eagle's nest
airy: breezy
affect [əˈfɛkt]: desire,
to influence
effect: result/to cause
affect: [əˈfɛkt] *verb*,
[ˈæfəkt] *noun*
against [əˈgɛnst]:
towards/opposing
aid [ˈeɪd]: to help
ade: beverage
aide: assistant
aide [ˈeɪd]: assistant
ade: beverage
aid: to help
air [ˈɛɚ]: atmosphere
e'er: ever
ere: eventually
err: mistake, stray
heir: inheritor
airy [ˈɛɚi]: breezy
aerie: eagle's nest
aisle [ˈaɪl]: walkway
isle: island
all [ˈɔl]: everything
awl: hand tool

31

allowed [əˈlaʊd]: permitted
aloud: out loud
ally: [əˈlaɪ] verb,
[ˈælaɪ] noun
aloud [əˈlaʊd]: out loud
allowed: permitted
altar [ˈɔltɚ]: ceremonial table
alter: to change
alter [ˈɔltɚ]: to change
altar: ceremonial table
anarchic [əˈnarkɪk]:
chaotic/self-organized
ant [ˈænt]: insect
aunt: parent's sister
ante [ˈæntɪ]: preliminary bet
auntie: parent's sister
apology [əˈpɔlədʒɪ]:
excuse/defense
appropriate:
[əˈproʊpriət] adj.,
[əˈproʊprieɪt] verb
arc [ˈark]: curve
ark: vessel
ark [ˈark]: vessel
arc: curve
articulate: [ərˈtɪkjuleɪt] verb,
[ərˈtɪkjulət] adj.
ascent [əˈsɛnt]: climb
assent: agreement

assent [əˈsɛnt]: agreement
ascent: climb
associate: [əˈsoʊsieɪt] verb,
[əˈsoʊsiət] noun
ate [ˈeɪt]: ingested
eight: 8
attribute: [əˈtrɪbjut] verb,
[ˈætrɪbjut] noun
auger [ˈɔgɚ]: drill
augur: to foretell
aught [ˈɔt]: all/nothing
ought: should
augur [ˈɔgɚ]: to foretell
auger: drill
aunt [ˈænt]: parent's sister
ant: insect
auntie [ˈæntɪ]: parent's sister
ante: preliminary bet
aural [ˈɔrəl]: of hearing
oral: of the mouth
auto [ˈɔtoʊ]: aotomobile
Otto: man's name
away [əˈweɪ]: absent
aweigh: of anchor clear of
the bottom
awed [ˈɔd]: in awe
odd: strange
aweful [ˈɔfʊl]: full of awe
awful: inspiring/revolting

**aweigh** [əˈweɪ]: of anchor
clear of the bottom
**away:** absent
**awesome** [ˈɔsəm]:
terrible/wonderful
**awful** [ˈɔfʊl]:
inspiring/revolting
**aweful:** full of awe
**awl** [ˈɔl]: hand tool
**all:** everything
**axel** [ˈæksl]: figure skating
term
**axle:** wheel
**axle** [ˈæksl]: wheel
**axel:** figure skating term
**aye** [ˈaɪ]: naval affirmative
**eye:** visual organ

# B

bail ['beɪl]: bucket handle
   bale: bundle of hay
bailed ['beɪld]: pumped
   baled: gathered into bails
bailey ['beɪlɪ]: outer wall of
   castle
   bailie: Scottish official
bailie ['beɪlɪ]: Scottish official
   bailey: outer wall of castle
bailing ['beɪlɪŋ]: pumping
   baling: wire
bait ['beɪt]: to torment
   bate: to lessen
baited ['beɪtəd]: tormented
   bated: lessened
baiting ['beɪtɪŋ]: tormenting
   bating: lessening
bald ['bɔld]: hairless
   balled: used a ball
   bawled: cried
bale ['beɪl]: bundle of hay
   bail: bucket handle
baled ['beɪld]:
   gathered into bails
   bailed: pumped

baling ['beɪlɪŋ]: wire
   bailing: pumping
ball ['bɔl]: sphere
   bawl: to cry
balled ['bɔld]: used a ball
   bald: hairless
   bawled: cried
band ['bænd]: group
   banned: forbidden
banned ['bænd]: forbidden
   band: group
bard ['bard]: poet
   barred: locked
bare ['bɛɚ]: naked
   bear: animal
bark ['bark]: of tree or dog
   barque: ship
barque ['bark]: ship
   bark: of tree or dog
barred ['bard]: locked
   bard: poet
Barry ['bɛrɪ]: man's name
   berry: fruit
base ['beɪs]: bottom
   bass: string instrument
based ['beɪst]: founded upon
   baste: drench, coat

35

bases ['beɪsəz]: foundations, bottoms

basses: string insturments

bask ['bæsk]: to savor

basque: bodice

Basque: Pyreneean ethnicity

basque ['bæsk]: bodice

bask: to savor

Basque: Pyreneean ethnicity

Basque ['bæsk]: Pyreneean ethnicity

bask: to savor

basque: bodice

bass ['beɪs]: string instrument

base: bottom

bass ['bæs]: fish

['beɪs] string instrument

basses ['beɪsəz]: string insturments

bases: foundations, bottoms

baste ['beɪst]: drench, coat

based: founded upon

bat ['bæt]: stick, flying mammal

batt: flat pad

bate ['beɪt]: to lessen

bait: to torment

bated ['beɪtəd]: lessened

baited: tormented

bating ['beɪtɪŋ]: lessening

baiting: tormenting

batt ['bæt]: flat pad

bat: stick, flying mammal

baud ['bɔd]: bits per second

bawd: brothel manager

bod: sexy body

bawd ['bɔd]: brothel manager

baud: bits per second

bod: sexy body

bawl ['bɔl]: to cry

ball: sphere

bawled ['bɔld]: cried

bald: hairless

balled: used a ball

bay ['beɪ]: cove, bark

bey: Turkish official

bays ['beɪz]: coves, barks

beize: green felt

beys: Turkish officials

beach ['bitʃ]: sandy shore

beech: tree

bear ['bɛɚ]: animal

bare: naked

beat ['bit]: to strike

beet: red root vegetable used in borscht

**beau** [ˈboʊ]: male friend
  **bow:** weapon that shoots
  arrows, bend
**beaut** [ˈbjut]: beauty
  **butte:** hill
**beech** [ˈbitʃ]: tree
  **beach:** sandy shore
**beer** [ˈbɪɚ]: malt beverage
  **bier:** coffin frame
**beet** [ˈbit]: red root vegetable
  used in borscht
  **beat:** to strike
**before** [bəˈfɔr]:
  in the past/in front of
**beize** [ˈbeɪz]: green felt
  **bays:** coves, barks
  **beys:** Turkish officials
**Bel** [ˈbɛl]: Babylonian god
  **bel:** Indian thorn tree
  **bell:** chime
  **belle:** beauty
**bel** [ˈbɛl]: Indian thorn tree
  **Bel:** Babylonian god
  **bell:** chime
  **belle:** beauty
**bell** [ˈbɛl]: chime
  **Bel:** Babylonian god
  **bel:** Indian thorn tree
  **belle:** beauty

**belle** [ˈbɛl]: beauty
  **Bel:** Babylonian god
  **bel:** Indian thorn tree
  **bell:** chime
**berry** [ˈbɛrɪ]: fruit
  **Barry:** man's name
**berth** [ˈbɚθ]: dockage
  **birth:** beginning
**besot** [bəˈsɔt]: to get drunk
  **besought:** implored
**besought** [bəˈsɔt]: implored
  **besot:** to get drunk
**better** [ˈbɛtɚ]: superior
  **bettor:** one who makes bets
**bettor** [ˈbɛtɚ]: one who
  makes bets
  **better:** superior
**bey** [ˈbeɪ]: Turkish official
  **bay:** cove, bark
**beys** [ˈbeɪz]: Turkish officials
  **bays:** coves, barks
  **beize:** green felt
**bier** [ˈbɪɚ]: coffin frame
  **beer:** malt beverage
**bight** [ˈbaɪt]: end of a rope
  **bite:** mouthful
  **byte:** 8 bits
**bill** [ˈbɪl]: payment/invoice

billed [ˈbɪld]: with a beak, invoiced
   build: to construct
birth [ˈbɚθ]: beginning
   berth: dockage
bit [ˈbɪt]: small piece, stung
   bitt: cleat
bite [ˈbaɪt]: mouthful
   bight: end of a rope
   byte: 8 bits
bitt [ˈbɪt]: cleat
   bit: small piece, stung
blew [ˈblu]: moved air
   blue: color
bloc [ˈblɔk]: alliance
   block: stop, cube
block [ˈblɔk]: stop, cube
   bloc: alliance
blond [ˈblɔnd]: light-haired man
   blonde: light-haired woman
blonde [ˈblɔnd]: light-haired woman
   blond: light-haired man
blue [ˈblu]: color
   blew: moved air
blunt [ˈblʌnt]: dull/pointed

boar [ˈbɔr]: wild pig
   Boer: Afrikaner
   boor: vulgar person
   bore: gave life, diameter, uninteresting person
board [ˈbɔrd]: plank
   bored: drilled out, not interested
boarder [ˈbɔrdɚ]: lodger
   border: boundary
bocks [ˈbɔks]: dark beers
   box: container
bod [ˈbɔd]: sexy body
   baud: bits per second
   bawd: brothel manager
bode [ˈboʊd]: omen
   bowed: bent
Boer [ˈbɔr]: Afrikaner
   boar: wild pig
   boor: vulgar person
   bore: gave life, diameter, uninteresting person
bold [ˈboʊld]: brave
   bowled: knocked over
bolder [ˈboʊldɚ]: braver
   boulder: large rock
bole [ˈboʊl]: trunk
   boll: seed pod
   bowl: dish

**boll** ['boʊl]: seed pod
  **bole:** trunk
  **bowl:** dish
**bolt** ['boʊlt]: secure/flee
**boned** ['boʊnd]:
  with/without bones
**boor** ['bɔr]: vulgar person
  **boar:** wild pig
  **Boer:** Afrikaner
  **bore:** gave life, diameter,
  uninteresting person
**boos** ['buz]: disapproval
  **booze:** distilled alcohol
**booze** ['buz]: distilled alcohol
  **boos:** disapproval
**border** ['bɔrdɚ]: boundary
  **boarder:** lodger
**bore** ['bɔr]: gave life, diameter,
  uninteresting person
  **boar:** wild pig
  **Boer:** Afrikaner
  **boor:** vulgar person
**bored** ['bɔrd]: drilled out, not
  interested
  **board:** plank
**born** ['bɔrn]: given life
  **borne:** carried
  **bourn:** stream boundary

**borne** ['bɔrn]: carried
  **born:** given life
  **bourn:** stream boundary
**borough** ['bɚoʊ]:
  municipality, township
  **burrow:** dig
**bough** ['baʊ]: tree branch
  **bow:** front, respectful nod
**boulder** ['boʊldɚ]: large rock
  **bolder:** braver
**bound** ['baʊnd]:
  moving/restrained
**bourn** ['bɔrn]: stream
  boundary
  **born:** given life
  **borne:** carried
**bow** ['boʊ]: weapon that
  shoots arrows, bend
  **beau:** male friend
**bow** ['baʊ]: front,
  respectful nod
  **bough:** tree branch
**bow:** ['boʊ] bend, ['baʊ] nod
**bowed** ['boʊd]: bent
  **bode:** omen
**bowl** ['boʊl]: dish
  **bole:** trunk
  **boll:** seed pod

**bowled** [ˈboʊld]: knocked over

**bold:** brave

**box** [ˈbɔks]: container

**bocks:** dark beers

**boy** [ˈbɔɪ]: male child

**buoy:** aid to navigation

**braid** [ˈbreɪd]: weave

**brayed:** cried like a donkey

**braise** [ˈbreɪz]: to cook in oil and water

**brays:** cries like a donkey

**braze:** solder with a copper alloy

**brake** [ˈbreɪk]: to slow down, stop

**break:** to split, pause, violate

**brayed** [ˈbreɪd]: cried like a donkey

**braid:** weave

**brays** [ˈbreɪz]: cries like a donkey

**braise:** to cook in oil and water

**braze:** solder with a copper alloy

**braze** [ˈbreɪz]: solder with a copper alloy

**braise:** to cook in oil and water

**brays:** cries like a donkey

**breach** [ˈbritʃ]: break through

**breech:** the back part

**bread** [ˈbrɛd]: baked goods

**bred:** mated/produced by mating

**break** [ˈbreɪk]: to split, pause, violate

**brake:** to slow down, stop

**bred** [ˈbrɛd]: mated/produced by mating

**bread:** baked goods

**breech** [ˈbritʃ]: the back part

**breach:** break through

**brewed** [ˈbrud]: fermented or steeped

**brood:** family

**brews** [ˈbruz]: beers

**bruise:** contusion

**bridal** [ˈbraɪdl]: for a wedding

**bridle:** halter, restraint, to show resentment

bridle ['braɪdl]: halter, restraint, to show resentment
 bridal: for a wedding
broach ['bhoʊtʃ]: to raise
 brooch: ornament
brooch ['bhoʊtʃ]: ornament
 broach: to raise
brood ['brud]: family
 brewed: fermented or steeped
brows ['braʊz]: forehead
 browse: to graze
browse ['braʊz]: to graze
 brows: forehead
bruise ['bruz]: contusion
 brews: beers
buckle ['bʌkl]: secure/collapse
build ['bɪld]: to construct
 billed: with a beak, invoiced
bundt ['bʌnt]: cake
 bunt: tap
bunt ['bʌnt]: tap
 bundt: cake
buoy ['bɔɪ]: aid to navigation
 boy: male child
burger ['bəgɚ]: hamburger
 burgher: merchant

burgher ['bəgɚ]: merchant
 burger: hamburger
burrow ['bəoʊ]: dig
 borough: municipality, township
bus ['bʌs]: coach
 buss: to kiss
buss ['bʌs]: to kiss
 bus: coach
bussed ['bʌst]: transported, kissed
 bust: sculpture
bust ['bʌst]: sculpture
 bussed: transported, kissed
butte ['bjut]: hill
 beaut: beauty
buy ['baɪ]: to purchase
 by: preposition
 bye: farewell
buyer ['baɪɚ]: purchaser
 byre: cow barn
by ['baɪ]: preposition
 buy: to purchase
 bye: farewell
bye ['baɪ]: farewell
 buy: to purchase
 by: preposition
byre ['baɪɚ]: cow barn
 buyer: purchaser

41

**byte** [ˈbaɪt]: 8 bits
   **bight:** end of a rope
   **bite:** mouthful

# C

C [ˈsi]: letter C
  sea: ocean
  see: to look
cache [ˈkæʃ]: store, stash
  cash: money
cached [ˈkæʃt]: stashed
  cashed: converted to cash
calendar [ˈkæləndɚ]:
  chart of days
  calender: paper press
calender [ˈkæləndɚ]:
  paper press
  calendar: chart of days
call [ˈkɔl]: to summon
  caul: amnionic membrane
  col: mountain pass
caller [ˈkɔlɚ]: visitor
  choler: yellow bile
  collar: worn around neck
can [ˈkæn]: metal container
  Cannes: city in France
can't [ˈkænt]: unable
  cant: bevel, jargon
Cannes [ˈkæn]: city in France
  can: metal container

cannon [ˈkænən]: gun
  canon: body of law
canon [ˈkænən]: body of law
  cannon: gun
cant [ˈkænt]: bevel, jargon
  can't: unable
canter [ˈkæntɚ]: gallop
  cantor: singer
cantor [ˈkæntɚ]: singer
  canter: gallop
canvas [ˈkænvəs]: fabric
  canvass: to solicit,
  gather opinions
canvass [ˈkænvəs]: to solicit,
  gather opinions
  canvas: fabric
capital [ˈkæpɪtəl]: seat of
  government
  capitol: main government
  building
capitol [ˈkæpɪtəl]: main
  government building
  capital: seat of government
carat [ˈkærət]: 200mg of
  precious stones
  karat: 1/24 fraction
  of pure gold
cash [ˈkæʃ]: money
  cache: store, stash

cashed [ˈkæʃt]: converted to cash
cached: stashed
cast [ˈkæst]: to throw, pour metal
caste: fixed social class
caste [ˈkæst]: fixed social class
cast: to throw, pour metal
caster [ˈkæstɚ]: thrower, small wheel (US)
castor: oil, small wheel (UK)
castor [ˈkæstɚ]: oil, small wheel (UK)
caster: thrower, small wheel (US)
caul [ˈkɔl]: amnionic membrane
call: to summon
col: mountain pass
cause [ˈkɔz]: reason
caws: cries of crows
caws [ˈkɔz]: cries of crows
cause: reason
cay [ˈki]: island
key: opens locks
quay: wharf
cedar [ˈsidɚ]: evergreen tree
seeder: one who plants seeds

cede [ˈsid]: to give
seed: add/remove seeds
seed: germ of a plant
ceding [ˈsidɪŋ]: giving
seeding: planting
ceiling [ˈsilɪŋ]: top of room
sealing: gluing shut
cell [ˈsɛl]: small room
sell: to exchange for money
cellar [ˈsɛlɚ]: space under a house
seller: one who sells
censer [ˈsɛnsɚ]: incense dish
censor: one who impedes free speech
sensor: detector
censor [ˈsɛnsɚ]: one who impedes free speech
censer: incense dish
sensor: detector
cent [ˈsɛnt]: 1/100th of a dollar
scent: smell
sent: dispatched
cents [ˈsɛnts]: 1/100ths of a dollar
scents: smells

44

cere [ˈsɪɚ-]: beak
  sear: to scorch
  seer: prophet
  sere: natural succession
cereal [ˈsɪrɪəl]: grain
  serial: in series
Ceres [ˈsiriz]: Roman goddess
  of agriculture
  series: sequence
certain [ˈsɚ-tən]:
  undefined/definite
cession [ˈsɛʃn]: giving up
  session: group meeting
chalk [ˈtʃɔk]: soft white rock
  chock: wedge
chamois: [ˈʃæmɪ] cloth,
  [ʃəmˈwa] sheep
chard [ˈtʃard]: spinach-like
  vegetable
  charred: burnt
charred [ˈtʃard]: burnt
  chard: spinach-like
  vegetable
chased [ˈtʃeɪst]: pursued
  chaste: celibate
chaste [ˈtʃeɪst]: celibate
  chased: pursued
cheap [ˈtʃip]: inexpensive
  cheep: peep

check [ˈtʃɛk]: payment/bill,
  tick mark, receipt,
  to examine
  Czech: Bohemian
cheep [ˈtʃip]: peep
  cheap: inexpensive
Chile [ˈtʃɪlɪ]: South American
  country
  chili: small red pepper
  chilly: cool
chili [ˈtʃɪlɪ]: small red pepper
  Chile: South American
  country
  chilly: cool
chilly [ˈtʃɪlɪ]: cool
  Chile: South American
  country
  chili: small red pepper
chock [ˈtʃɔk]: wedge
  chalk: soft white rock
choir [ˈkwaɪɚ-]: singers
  quire: 1/20 of a ream of
  paper
choler [ˈkɔlɚ-]: yellow bile
  caller: visitor
  collar: worn around neck
choral [ˈkɔrəl]: composition
  sung by a chorus
  coral: marine polyps

45

chorale [kəˈræl]: choir
  corral: horse pen
chord [ˈkɔrd]: line, group
  of notes
  cord: rope
  cored: with/without a core
chute [ˈʃut]: inclined trough,
  parachute
  shoot: fire a weapon
cite [ˈsaɪt]: to reference
  sight: vision
  site: location
cited [ˈsaɪtəd]: referred to
  sighted: seen, able to see
  sited: located
cites [ˈsaɪts]: refers to
  sights: sees, views
  sites: locates
clack [ˈklæk]: chatter
  claque: group
  of sycophants
claque [ˈklæk]:
  group of sycophants
  clack: chatter
clause [ˈklɔz]: section
  of contract
  claws: nails
  Klaus: Santa

claws [ˈklɔz]: nails
  clause: section of contract
  Klaus: Santa
cleave [ˈkliv]: adhere/separate
clew [ˈklu]: aft corner of a sail
  clue: hint
click [ˈklɪk]: tick
  clique: exclusive group
climb [ˈklaɪm]: ascend
  clime: climate
clime [ˈklaɪm]: climate
  climb: ascend
clip [ˈklɪp]: fasten/detach
clique [ˈklɪk]: exclusive group
  click: tick
close: [ˈklouz] *verb*,
  [ˈklous] *adj./adv.*
clue [ˈklu]: hint
  clew: aft corner of a sail
coal [ˈkoʊl]: fossil fuel
  cole: plant of crucifer family
coaled [ˈkoʊld]: fueled
  with coal
  cold: low temperature
coarse [ˈkɔrs]: rough
  course: path
coat [ˈkoʊt]: outer garment,
  finish
  cote: small animal shed

coax ['kouks]: to persuade
cokes: sugary beverages
cocks ['kɔks]: roosters
cox: steersman
Cox: variety of apple
coddling ['kɔdlɪŋ]: spoiling
through preferential
treatment
codling: unripe apple
codling ['kɔdlɪŋ]: unripe
apple
coddling: spoiling through
preferential treatment
coffer ['kɔfɚ]: strongbox
cougher: one who coughs
coin ['kɔɪn]: money
quoin: cornerstone
cokes ['kouks]: sugary
beverages
coax: to persuade
col ['kɔl]: mountain pass
call: to summon
caul: amnionic membrane
cold ['kould]: low temperature
coaled: fueled with coal
cole ['koul]: plant of crucifer
family
coal: fossil fuel

collar ['kɔlɚ]: worn
around neck
caller: visitor
choler: yellow bile
colonel ['kɚnəl]: military
officer
kernel: seed
combine: [kəm'baɪn] verb,
['kɔmbaɪn] noun
commencement
[kə'mɛnsmənt]:
beginning/ completion
complement ['kɔmpləmənt]:
quantity
compliment: praise
complex: [kəm'plɛks] adj.,
['kɔmpləks] noun
compliment ['kɔmpləmənt]:
praise
complement: quantity
compound: ['kɔmpaund]
noun, [kəm'paund] verb
comprise [kəm'praɪz]: part,
whole
conch ['kɔŋk]: marine
mollusk
conk: blow to the head
concrete: [kən'krit] adj.,
['kɔnkrit] noun

**conduct:** [ˈkɒndəkt] *noun,*
  [kənˈdʌkt] *verb*
**conk** [ˈkɒŋk]: blow to the head
  **conch:** marine mollusk
**constrain** [kənˈstreɪn]:
  force/contain
**construct:** [kənˈstrʌkt] *verb,*
  [ˈkɒnstrəkt] *noun*
**consult** [kənˈsʌlt]:
  give/take advice
**consult:** [kənˈsʌlt] *verb,*
  [ˈkɒnsəlt] *noun*
**content:** [ˈkɒntənt] *noun,*
  [kəˈnwɛnt] *verb*
**contest:** [ˈkɒntəst] *noun,*
  [kənˈtɛst] *verb*
**contingent** [kənˈtɪndʒənt]:
  certain/uncertain
**continue** [kənˈtɪnju]:
  resume/postpone
**contract:** [kənˈtrækt] *verb,*
  [ˈkɒntrətk] *noun*
**contrast:** [ˈkɒntrəst] *noun,*
  [kənˈtræst] *verb*
**converse:** [ˈkɒnvɚs] *noun,*
  [kənˈvɚs] *verb*
**convert:** [kənˈvɚt] *verb,*
  [ˈkɒnvɚt] *noun*

**convict:** [ˈkɒnvɪkt] *noun,*
  [kənˈvɪkt] *verb*
**coo** [ˈku]: to murmur
  **coup:** blow, overthrow
**copped** [ˈkɒpt]: arrested
  **Copt:** Egyptian to a Roman
**cops** [ˈkɒps]: police officers
  (US)
  **copse:** stand of trees
**copse** [ˈkɒps]: stand of trees
  **cops:** police officers (US)
**Copt** [ˈkɒpt]: Egyptian to a
  Roman
  **copped:** arrested
**coral** [ˈkɒrəl]: marine polyps
  **choral:** composition sung by
  a chorus
**cord** [ˈkɔrd]: rope
  **chord:** line, group of notes
  **cored:** with/without a core
**core** [ˈkɔr]: inner part
  **corps:** organized group
**cored** [ˈkɔrd]: with/without
  a core
  **chord:** line, group of notes
  **cord:** rope
**corps** [ˈkɔr]: organized group
  **core:** inner part

corral [kəˈræl]: horse pen
chorale: choir
cote [ˈkoʊt]: small animal shed
coat: outer garment, finish
cougher [ˈkɔfɚ]: one who coughs
coffer: strongbox
council [ˈkaʊnsəl]: official group
counsel: advice
counsel [ˈkaʊnsəl]: advice
council: official group
coup [ˈku]: blow, overthrow
coo: to murmur
course [ˈkɔrs]: path
coarse: rough
cox [ˈkɔks]: steersman
cocks: roosters
Cox: variety of apple
Cox [ˈkɔks]: variety of apple
cocks: roosters
cox: steersman
craft [ˈkræft]: manual occupation
kraft: strong paper
crater [ˈkreɪtɚ]: impact hole, mouth of volcano
krater: ancient Greek jar

creak [ˈkrik]: squeak
creek: stream
creek [ˈkrik]: stream
creak: squeak
crewed [ˈkrud]: manned
crude: coarse
crews [ˈkruz]: more than one crew
cruise: sea voyage
critical [ˈkrɪtɪkəl]: essential/disapproving
croc [ˈkrɔk]: crocodile
crock: pot
crock [ˈkrɔk]: pot
croc: crocodile
crude [ˈkrud]: coarse
crewed: manned
cruise [ˈkruz]: sea voyage
crews: more than one crew
cue [ˈkju]: signal
Kew: Gardens in London
queue: waiting line
curser [ˈkɚsɚ]: one who curses
cursor: indicator
cursor [ˈkɚsɚ]: indicator
curser: one who curses
custom [ˈkastəm]: common/special

49

**cygnet** [ˈsɪgnət]: young swan
  **signet:** authenticating seal
**Czech** [ˈtʃɛk]: Bohemian
  **check:** payment/bill, tick
  mark, receipt, to examine

# D

dam [ˈdæm]: waterworks
  damn: curse
dammed [ˈdæmd]: prevented
  from flowing
  damned: cursed
damn [ˈdæm]: curse
  dam: waterworks
damned [ˈdæmd]: cursed
  dammed: prevented
  from flowing
days [ˈdeɪz]: more than
  one day
  daze: bewilder
daze [ˈdeɪz]: bewilder
  days: more than one day
dear [ˈdɪɚ]: beloved
  deer: animal
decrease: [dəˈkris] verb,
  [ˈdikris] noun
deer [ˈdɪɚ]: animal
  dear: beloved
defect: [ˈdifəkt] noun,
  [dəˈfɛkt] verb
defense: [ˈdifəns] used in
  US football,
  [dəˈfɛns] military

degenerate:
  [dəˈdʒɛnɚət] noun,
  [dəˈdʒɛnɚeɪt] verb
deliberate: [dəˈlɪbɚeɪt] verb,
  [dəˈlɪbɚət] adj.
derivation [dərɪˈveɪsən]:
  original/unoriginal
desert [dəˈzɚt]: abandon
  dessert: sweets
desert: [ˈdɛzɚt] noun,
  [dəˈzɚt] verb
dessert [dəˈzɚt]: sweets
  desert: abandon
detail: [dəˈteɪl] verb,
  [ˈditeɪl] noun
dew [ˈdju]: condensation
  due: payable
dews [ˈdjuz]: condensation
  dues: payments
Di [ˈdaɪ]: short for Diana
  die: to become dead
  dye: pigment
die [ˈdaɪ]: to become dead
  Di: short for Diana
  dye: pigment
died [ˈdaɪd]: became dead
  dyed: pigmented
dies [ˈdaɪz]: becomes dead
  dyes: pigments

dike ['daɪk]: wall/ditch

dine ['daɪn]: have dinner

dyne: unit of energy

dire ['daɪɚ]: desperate

dyer: one who uses dyes

discharge: ['dɪstʃərdʒ] *noun*,
['dɪs'tʃardʒ] *verb*

discount: ['dɪskaʊnt] *noun*,
[dɪs'kaʊnt] *verb*

discreet [dɪs'krit]: confidential

discrete: individual

discrete [dɪs'krit]: individual

discreet: confidential

discursive [dɪs'kɚ-sɪv]:
directed/directionless

disposed [dɪs'poʊzd]:
available/discarded

dispute: ['dɪspjut] *noun*,
[dɪspj'ut] *verb*

divers [daɪv'ɚ-s]: several

diverse: varied

divers [daɪv'ɚ-s] *adj*.
[d'aɪvɚz] *noun*

diverse [daɪə'ɚ-s]: varied

divers: several

do ['doʊ]: musical note C

doe: female deer

dough: unbaked bread

do: ['doʊ] note,
['du] to do, hairdo

doc ['dɔk]: medic

dock: berth

dock ['dɔk]: berth

doc: medic

doe ['doʊ]: female deer

do: musical note C

dough: unbaked bread

does ['doʊz]: more than
one female deer

dos: more than one note C

dose: quantity of medicine

doughs: more than
one dough

doze: to nap

does: ['doʊz] notes, more
than one female deer
['dʌz] 3ps of "to do"

dollop ['dɔləp]:
large/small amount

done ['dʌn]: completed

dun: grey-brown

**dos** ['doʊz]: more than one note C
**does:** more than one female deer
**dose:** quantity of medicine
**doughs:** more than one dough
**doze:** to nap
**dos:** ['doʊz] notes, ['duz] hairdos
**dose** ['doʊz]: quantity of medicine
**does:** more than one female deer
**dos:** more than one note C
**doughs:** more than one dough
**doze:** to nap
**dough** ['doʊ]: unbaked bread
**do:** musical note C
**doe:** female deer
**doughs** ['doʊz]: more than one dough
**does:** more than one female deer
**dos:** more than one note C
**dose:** quantity of medicine
**doze:** to nap

**dove:** ['dʌv] *noun*, ['doʊv] *verb*
**downhill** [daʊn'hɪl]: better/worse
**doze** ['doʊz]: to nap
**does:** more than one female deer
**dos:** more than one note C
**dose:** quantity of medicine
**doughs:** more than one dough
**draft** ['dræft]: version of a manuscript, beer on tap
**draught:** of wind, boat, portion of drink
**draught** ['dræft]: of wind, boat, portion of drink
**draft:** version of a manuscript, beer on tap
**due** ['dju]: payable
**dew:** condensation
**dues** ['djuz]: payments
**dews:** condensation
**dun** ['dʌn]: grey-brown
**done:** completed
**dust** ['dʌst]: add /remove dust
**dusted** ['dʌstəd]: with/without dust

**dye** ['daɪ]: pigment
  **Di:** short for Diana
  **die:** to become dead
**dyed** ['daɪd]: pigmented
  **died:** became dead
**dyeing** ['daɪɪŋ]: pigmenting
  **dying:** near death
**dyer** ['daɪɚ]: one who uses
  pigments
  **dire:** desperate
**dyes** ['daɪz]: pigments
  **dies:** becomes dead
**dying** ['daɪɪŋ]: near death
  **dyeing:** pigmenting
**dyne** ['daɪn]: unit of energy
  **dine:** have dinner

# E

e'er ['ɛɚ]: ever
air: atmosphere
ere: eventually
err: mistake, stray
heir: inheritor
earn ['ɚn]: to make money
urn: jar
effect [əˈfɛkt]: result/to cause
affect: desire, to influence
eight ['eɪt]: 8
ate: ingested
either ['aɪðɚ]: one of/both
elaborate: [əˈlæbɚət] adj.,
   [əˈlæbɚeɪt] verb
elude [ɪˈlud]: to avoid
illude: to deceive
endure [əˈndjuɚ]:
   undergo/abide
enjoin [əˈndʒɔɪn]:
   impose/prohibit
entrance: [ənˈtræns] verb,
   ['ɛntrəns] noun

ere ['ɛɚ]: eventually
air: atmosphere
e'er: ever
err: mistake, stray
heir: inheritor
err ['ɛɚ]: mistake, stray
air: atmosphere
e'er: ever
ere: eventually
heir: inheritor
estimate: ['ɛstɪmət] noun,
   ['ɛstɪmeɪt] verb
eunuchs ['junɪks]: castrated
   men
UNIX: operating system
evening: ['ivənɪŋ] verb,
   ['ivnɪŋ] noun
ewe ['ju]: sheep
yew: tree
you: 2nd person pronoun
ewes ['juz]: sheep
use: to apply
yews: trees
execute ['ɛgzəkjut]:
   initiate/terminate

**eye** [ˈaɪ]: visual organ
   **aye:** naval affirmative
**eyelet** [ˈaɪlət]: hole for
   shoelaces
   **islet:** small island

# F

fain ['feɪn]: willing
    feign: to pretend
faint ['feɪnt]: to pass out
    feint: misdirection
fair ['fɛɚ]: just, light
    fare: payment for travel,
    food, to get by
fairing ['fɛrɪŋ]: streamlining
    faring: traveling
fairy ['fɛrɪ]: magical person
    ferry: passenger vessel
faker ['feɪkɚ]: deceiver
    fakir: Hindu ascetic
fakir ['feɪkɚ]: Hindu ascetic
    faker: deceiver
fare ['fɛɚ]: payment for
    travel, food, to get by
    fair: just, light
faring ['fɛrɪŋ]: traveling
    fairing: streamlining
farrow ['fɛroʊ]: litter of pigs
    pharaoh: Ancient Egyptian
    emperor
fast ['fæst]: quick/unmoving
faux ['foʊ]: fake
    foe: enemy

fay ['feɪ]: fairy
    Faye: woman's name
    fey: strange
Faye ['feɪ]: woman's name
    fay: fairy
    fey: strange
fays ['feɪz]: fairies
    faze: stun
    phase: part of a sequence
faze ['feɪz]: stun
    fays: fairies
    phase: part of a sequence
feat ['fit]: accomplishment
    feet: more than one foot
feet ['fit]: more than one foot
    feat: accomplishment
feign ['feɪn]: to pretend
    fain: willing
feint ['feɪnt]: misdirection
    faint: to pass out
ferry ['fɛrɪ]: passenger vessel
    fairy: magical person
few ['fju]: not many
    phew: expression of relief
fey ['feɪ]: strange
    fay: fairy
    Faye: woman's name
file ['faɪl]: filder, hand tool
    phial: small glass bottle

fill [ˈfɪl]: make full
  Phil: short for "Philip"
fillet: [ˈfɪlət] joint
  reinforcement,
  [fiˈleɪ] cut of meat/fish
filter [ˈfɪltɚ]: screen
  philter: love potion
find [ˈfaɪnd]: to locate
  fined: penalized
fine [ˈfaɪn]: excellent/passable
fined [ˈfaɪnd]: penalized
  find: to locate
finish [ˈfɪnɪʃ]: completion
  Finnish: of Finland
finished [ˈfɪnɪʃt]:
  complete/destroyed
Finnish [ˈfɪnɪʃ]: of Finland
  finish: completion
fir [ˈfɚ]: evergreen tree
  fur: animal hair
  furr: separate with wood
  strips
fisher [ˈfɪʃɚ]: fisherman
  fissure: crack
fissure [ˈfɪʃɚ]: crack
  fisher: fisherman
fix [ˈfɪks]: repair/castrate

flair [ˈflɛɚ]: natural ability
  flare: distress signal,
  widening
flare [ˈflɛɚ]: distress signal,
  widening
  flair: natural ability
flea [ˈfli]: jumping, biting insect
  flee: to escape
flecks [ˈflɛks]: specs
  flex: to bend
flee [ˈfli]: to escape
  flea: jumping, biting insect
flew [ˈflu]: moved or traveled
  by air
  flu: influenza
  flue: chimney
flex [ˈflɛks]: to bend
  flecks: specs
Flo [ˈfloʊ]: short for "Florence"
  floe: floating sheet of ice
  flow: movement of liquid
flocks [ˈflɔks]: groups of birds
  phlox: scented plant
floe [ˈfloʊ]: floating sheet
  of ice
  Flo: short for "Florence"
  flow: movement of liquid
flog [ˈflɔg]: promote/criticize

**flour** [ˈflaʊɚ]: milled grain
  **flower:** blossom
**flow** [ˈfloʊ]: movement
  of liquid
  **Flo:** short for "Florence"
  **floe:** floating sheet of ice
**flower** [ˈflaʊɚ]: blossom
  **flour:** milled grain
**flu** [ˈflu]: influenza
  **flew:** moved or traveled
  by air
  **flue:** chimney
**flue** [ˈflu]: chimney
  **flew:** moved or traveled
  by air
  **flu:** influenza
**foe** [ˈfoʊ]: enemy
  **faux:** fake
**for** [ˈfɔr]: not against
  **fore:** in front
  **four:** 4
**fore** [ˈfɔr]: in front
  **for:** not against
  **four:** 4
**forego** [fərˈgoʊ]: to precede
  **forgo:** to abstain
**foreword** [ˈfɔrwɚd]:
  introduction
  **forward:** ahead

**forge** [ˈfɔrdʒ]:
  strengthen/counterfeit
**forgo** [fərˈgoʊ]: to abstain
  **forego:** to precede
**fort** [ˈfɔrt]: fortification
  **forte:** strong point
**forte** [ˈfɔrt]: strong point
  **fort:** fortification
**forth** [ˈfɔrθ]: forward
  **fourth:** 4th
**forward** [ˈfɔrwɚd]: ahead
  **foreword:** introduction
**foul** [ˈfaʊl]: polluted, offensive
  **fowl:** poultry
**four** [ˈfɔr]: 4
  **for:** not against
  **fore:** in front
**fourth** [ˈfɔrθ]: 4th
  **forth:** forward
**fowl** [ˈfaʊl]: poultry
  **foul:** polluted, offensive
**frees** [ˈfriz]: releases
  **freeze:** cold spell
  **frieze:** wall decoration
**freeze** [ˈfriz]: cold spell
  **frees:** releases
  **frieze:** wall decoration
**friar** [ˈfraɪɚ]: monk
  **fryer:** chicken

**frieze** [ˈfriz]: wall decoration
   **frees:** releases
   **freeze:** cold spell
**fryer** [ˈfraɪɚ]: chicken
   **friar:** monk
**fur** [ˈfɚ]: animal hair
   **fir:** evergreen tree
   **furr:** separate with
   wood strips
**furr** [ˈfɚ]: separate with
   wood strips
   **fir:** evergreen tree
   **fur:** animal hair

# G

gaff ['gæf]: spear, spar
  gaffe: mistake
gaffe ['gæf]: mistake
  gaff: spear, spar
gait ['geɪt]: manner of walking
  or running
  gate: fence door
gall ['gɔl]: bile
  Gaul: Roman France
garnish ['garnɪʃ]:
  provide/deprive
gate ['geɪt]: fence door
  gait: manner of walking
  or running
Gaul ['gɔl]: Roman France
  gall: bile
gays ['geɪz]: homosexuals
  gaze: stare
gaze ['geɪz]: stare
  gays: homosexuals
generally ['dʒɛnə-əlɪ]:
  sometimes/always
genes ['dʒinz]: chromosomes
  jeans: pants

gild ['gɪld]: to cover with gold
  gilled: having gills
  guild: society of craftsmen
gilled ['gɪld]: having gills
  gild: to cover with gold
  guild: society of craftsmen
gilt ['gɪlt]: gold-plated
  guilt: culpability
give out ['gɪv 'aʊt]:
  provide/run out
gnawed ['nɔd]: chewed
  nod: head tilt
gneiss ['naɪs]:
  coarse-grained rock
  nice: pleasant
go ['goʊ]: pass/fail
gored ['gɔrd]: injured with
  horns or tusks
  gourd: hollow
  hard-shelled fruit
gorilla [gə-'ɪlə]: large ape
  guerrilla: paramilitary
  group
gourd ['gɔrd]: hollow
  hard-shelled fruit
  gored: injured with horns
  or tusks
grade ['greɪd]: slope
  grayed: turned gray

61

grade ['greɪd]: slope/level
graduate: ['grædʒueɪt] *verb*,
['grædʒjuət] *noun*
graft ['græft]: transplant
graphed: plotted
graphed ['græft]: plotted
graft: transplant
grate ['greɪt]: latticed
ironwork
great: very good or large
grayed ['greɪd]: turned gray
grade: slope
grays ['greɪz]: tones of gray
graze: to eat grass
graze ['greɪz]: to eat grass
grays: tones of gray
grease ['gris]: cooking fat,
lubricant
Greece: Mediterranean
country
great ['greɪt]: very good
or large
grate: latticed ironwork
greave ['griv]: leg armor
grieve: to mourn
greaves ['grivz]: leg armor
grieves: mourns

Greece ['gris]:
Mediterranean country
grease: cooking fat,
lubricant
grieve ['griv]: to mourn
greave: leg armor
grieves ['grivz]: mourns
greaves: leg armor
grill ['grɪl]: barbecue
grille: latticework
grille ['grɪl]: latticework
grill: barbecue
groan ['groʊn]: complaining
grown: become bigger
grown ['groʊn]:
become bigger
groan: complaining
guerrilla [gɚ'ɪlə]:
paramilitary group
gorilla: large ape
guild ['gɪld]: society of
craftsmen
gild: to cover with gold
gilled: having gills
guilt ['gɪlt]: culpability
gilt: gold-plated
guise ['gaɪz]: appearance
guys: fellows

**guys** [ˈgaɪz]: fellows
   **guise:** appearance
**gym** [ˈdʒɪm]: gymnasium
   **Jim:** short for "James"

# H

hail [ˈheɪl]: ice
  hale: healthy
hair [ˈhɛɚ]: fiber
  hare: rabbit
hale [ˈheɪl]: healthy
  hail: ice
halve [ˈhæv]: break in two
  have: possess
halves [ˈhævz]: more than a
  single half
  haves: the rich
handicap [ˈhændɪkˈæp]:
  advantage/disadvantage
hangar [ˈhæŋɚ]: garage
  for airplanes
  hanger: hook
hanger [ˈhæŋɚ]: hook
  hangar: garage
  for airplanes
hare [ˈhɛɚ]: rabbit
  hair: fiber
hart [ˈhart]: stag
  heart: blood pump
haut [ˈoʊ]: high
  oh: interjection
  owe: be indebted

have [ˈhæv]: possess
  halve: break in two
haves [ˈhævz]: the rich
  halves: more than a single
  half
hay [ˈheɪ]: dried grass
  hey: exclamation
hays [ˈheɪz]: dried grasses
  haze: poor visibility
haze [ˈheɪz]: poor visibility
  hays: dried grasses
he'll [ˈhil]: he will
  heal: cure
  heel: hind part of foot
heal [ˈhil]: cure
  he'll: he will
  heel: hind part of foot
hear [ˈhɪɚ]: listen
  here: not there
heard [ˈhɚd]: listened
  herd: group of animals
heart [ˈhart]: blood pump
  hart: stag
heel [ˈhil]: hind part of foot
  he'll: he will
  heal: cure

heir ['ɛɚ]: inheritor
air: atmosphere
e'er: ever
ere: eventually
err: mistake, stray
help ['hɛlp]: assist/prevent
herd ['hɚd]: group of animals
heard: listened
here ['hɪɚ]: not there
hear: listen
heroin ['hɛroʊɪn]:
opiate drug
heroine: female hero
heroine ['hɛroʊɪn]: female
hero
heroin: opiate drug
hew ['hju]: split/join
hue: tint
Hugh: man's name
hey ['heɪ]: exclamation
hay: dried grass
hi ['haɪ]: greeting
high: tall
hide ['haɪd]: animal skin
hied: hurried
hied ['haɪd]: hurried
hide: animal skin
high ['haɪ]: tall
hi: greeting

higher ['haɪɚ]: opposite
of lower
hire: employ
hire ['haɪɚ]: employ
higher: opposite of lower
ho ['hoʊ]: exclamation
hoe: farming tool
hoar ['hɔr]: white frost
whore: prostitute
hoard ['hɔrd]: store or stock
of value
horde: crowd
whored: prostituted
hoarse ['hɔrs]: rough voice
horse: animal
hoe ['hoʊ]: farming tool
ho: exclamation
hoes ['hoʊz]: farming tools
hose: flexible pipe
hold ['hoʊld]: to grip
holed: having a hole
hold up ['hoʊld 'ʌp]:
support/impede
hole ['hoʊl]: perforation, pit
whole: entire
holed ['hoʊld]: having a hole
hold: to grip

holey [ˈhoʊlɪ]: perforated
  holy: sacred
  wholly: entirely
holy [ˈhoʊlɪ]: sacred
  holey: perforated
  wholly: entirely
horde [ˈhɔrd]: crowd
  hoard: store or stock
  of value
  whored: prostituted
horse [ˈhɔrs]: animal
  hoarse: rough voice
hose [ˈhoʊz]: flexible pipe
  hoes: farming tools
hour [ˈaʊɚ]: unit of time
  our: belonging to us
hours [ˈaʊɚz]: units of time
  ours: belonging to us
house: [ˈhaʊs] *noun*,
  [ˈhaʊz] *verb*
hue [ˈhju]: tint
  hew: split/join
  Hugh: man's name
Hugh [ˈhju]: man's name
  hew: split/join
  hue: tint

humerus [ˈhjumɚus]:
  funny bone
  humorous: funny
humorous [ˈhjumɚus]: funny
  humerus: funny bone

# I

illude [ɪˈlud]: to deceive
   elude: to avoid
inc [ˈɪŋk]: incorporated
   ink: writing fluid
incomparable [ɪˈnkɔmpərəbl]:
   matchless/mismatched
increase: [ˈɪnkris] *noun*,
   [ɪˈnkris] *verb*
ink [ˈɪŋk]: writing fluid
   inc: incorporated
inns [ˈɪnz]: hotels
   ins: and outs
ins [ˈɪnz]: and outs
   inns: hotels
insert: [ˈɪnsə-t] *noun*,
   [ɪnˈsə-t] *verb*
inside: [ɪˈnsaɪd] *adv.*,
   [ˈɪnsaɪd] *noun*
intimate: [ˈɪntɪmət] *adj.*,
   [ˈɪntɪmeɪt] adj.
invalid: [ˈɪnvalɪd] *noun.*,
   [ɪnˈvælɪd] *adj.*
isle [ˈaɪl]: island
   aisle: walkway
islet [ˈaɪlət]: small island
   eyelet: hole for shoelaces

it's [ˈɪts]: it is
   its: whose?
its [ˈɪts]: whose?
   it's: it is

# J

jam [ˈdʒæm]: squeeze
    **jamb:** side post of doorway
jamb [ˈdʒæm]: side post
    of doorway
    **jam:** squeeze
jeans [ˈdʒinz]: pants
    **genes:** chromosomes
jewel [ˈdʒul]: precious stone
    **joule:** unit of energy
Jim [ˈdʒɪm]: short for "James"
    **gym:** gymnasium
joule [ˈdʒul]: unit of energy
    **jewel:** precious stone

# K

karat ['kærət]: 1/24 fraction
of pure gold
carat: 200mg of precious
stones
kernel ['kɚ-nəl]: seed
colonel: military officer
Kew ['kju]: Gardens in London
cue: signal
queue: waiting line
key ['ki]: opens locks
cay: island
quay: wharf
Klaus ['klɔz]: Santa
clause: section of contract
claws: nails
knap ['næp]: break with
a hammer, crest of a hill
nap: short sleep
knead ['nid]: work dough
need: require
knew ['nju]: was informed
new: opposite of old
knickers ['nɪkɚ-z]: women's
underwear
nickers: those who nick

knight ['naɪt]: honorary title
night: darkness
knit ['nɪt]: to make garments
out of yarn
nit: louse egg
knits ['nɪts]: does knitting
nits: louse eggs
knob ['nɔb]: handle
nob: rich person
knock ['nɔk]: to rap
nock: notch in an arrow
knot ['nɔt]: fastening
naught: nothing
nought: zero
know ['noʊ]: to be informed
no: negative
Noh: Japanese masked
drama
knows ['noʊz]: is informed
noes: votes against
nose: part of face
kraft ['kræft]: strong paper
craft: manual occupation
krater ['kreɪtɚ-]: ancient
Greek jar
crater: impact hole,
mouth of volcano

# L

lacks ['læks]: is missing
  lax: undisciplined
lain ['leɪn]: was laying
  lane: narrow street
lam ['læm]: escape
  lamb: baby sheep
lama ['lamə]: Buddhist
  preacher
  llama: pack animal
lamb ['læm]: baby sheep
  lam: escape
lane ['leɪn]: narrow street
  lain: was laying
lax ['læks]: undisciplined
  lacks: is missing
lay ['leɪ]: recline
  lei: flower necklace
lays ['leɪz]: does lay
  laze: be lazy
  leis: flower necklaces
laze ['leɪz]: be lazy
  lays: does lay
  leis: flower necklaces
lea ['li]: meadow
  lee: downwind
  li: 0.5km in China

leach ['litʃ]: wash out
  leech: bloodsucking parasite
lead ['lɛd]: heavy grey metal
  led: did not follow
lead: ['lid] not to follow
  ['lɛd] heavy grey metal
leading: ['lidɪŋ] in the lead
  ['lɛdɪŋ] space between lines
leak ['lɪk]: escape of liquid
  leek: variety of onion
lean ['lin]: not fat,
  rest at an angle
  lien: claim on property
leas ['liz]: meadows
  lees: dregs
lease ['lis]: provide/receive
leased ['list]: rented
  least: minimally
least ['list]: minimally
  leased: rented
led ['lɛd]: did not follow
  lead: heavy grey metal
lee ['li]: downwind
  lea: meadow
  li: 0.5km in China
leech ['litʃ]: bloodsucking
  parasite
  leach: wash out

leek [ˈlɪk]: variety of onion
leak: escape of liquid
lees [ˈliz]: dregs
leas: meadows
left [ˈlɛft]: remained/departed
lei [ˈleɪ]: flower necklace
lay: recline
leis [ˈleɪz]: flower necklaces
lays: does lay
laze: be lazy
lessen [ˈlɛsən]: to decrease
lesson: instruction
lesson [ˈlɛsən]: instruction
lessen: to decrease
li [ˈli]: 0.5km in China
lea: meadow
lee: downwind
liar [ˈlaɪɚ]: one who lies
lyre: harp
lichen [ˈlaɪkən]: fungus
liken: compare
licker [ˈlɪkɚ]: one who licks
liquor: distilled alcoholic
beverage
lie [ˈlaɪ]: untruth
lye: caustic substance
liege [ˈliʒ]: lord/vassal

lien [ˈlin]: claim on property
lean: not fat,
rest at an angle
lieu [ˈlu]: instead
loo: toilet (UK)
Lou: short for Louis
lightening [ˈlaɪtnɪŋ]:
making lighter
lightning: flash in the sky
lightning [ˈlaɪtnɪŋ]:
flash in the sky
lightening: making lighter
liken [ˈlaɪkən]: compare
lichen: fungus
limb [ˈlɪm]: arm or leg, branch
limn: to illuminate
limbs [ˈlɪmz]: arms or legs,
branches
limns: illuminates
limn [ˈlɪm]: to illuminate
limb: arm or leg, branch
limns [ˈlɪmz]: illuminates
limbs: arms
links [ˈlɪŋks]: connections
lynx: wild cat
liquor [ˈlɪkɚ]: distilled
alcoholic beverage
licker: one who licks

**literal** [ˈlɪtə-əl]: direct meaning
  **littoral:** coastal
**literally** [ˈlɪtə-əlɪ]: actually/virtually
**littoral** [ˈlɪtə-əl]: coastal
  **literal:** direct meaning
**live:** [ˈlɪv] *verb*, [ˈlaɪv] *adj.*
**llama** [ˈlamə]: pack animal
  **lama:** Buddhist preacher
**lo** [ˈloʊ]: *interjection*
  **low:** not high
**load** [ˈloʊd]: cargo
  **lode:** mineral vein
  **lowed:** mooed
**loan** [ˈloʊn]: borrowing
  **lone:** by itself
**loath** [ˈloʊθ]: reluctant, unwilling
  **loathe:** to hate
**loathe** [ˈloʊθ]: to hate
  **loath:** reluctant, unwilling
**loch** [ˈlɔk]: lake
  **lock:** security device, strand of hair
**lochs** [ˈlɔks]: lakes
  **locks:** security devices, strands of hair
  **lox:** smoked salmon

**lock** [ˈlɔk]: security device, strand of hair
  **loch:** lake
**locks** [ˈlɔks]: security devices, strands of hair
  **lochs:** lakes
  **lox:** smoked salmon
**lode** [ˈloʊd]: mineral vein
  **load:** cargo
  **lowed:** mooed
**lone** [ˈloʊn]: by itself
  **loan:** borrowing
**loo** [ˈlu]: British toilet
  **lieu:** instead
  **Lou:** short for Louis
**loon** [ˈlun]: water fowl
  **lune:** crescent shape
**loop** [ˈlup]: circular pattern
  **loupe:** magnifying glass
**loos** [ˈluz]: toilets (UK)
  **lose:** fail to win
**loot** [ˈlut]: booty
  **lute:** stringed instrument
**lose** [ˈluz]: fail to win
  **loos:** British toilets
**Lot** [ˈlɔt]: Biblical character
  **lot:** plot of land, quantity
**lot** [ˈlɔt]: plot of land, quantity
  **Lot:** Biblical character

**Lot's** [ˈlɔts]: Biblical character's
   **lots:** plots of land, quantities
**lots** [ˈlɔts]: plots of land, quantities
   **Lot's:** Biblical character's
**Lou** [ˈlu]: short for Louis
   **lieu:** instead
   **loo:** toilet (UK)
**loupe** [ˈlup]: magnifying glass
   **loop:** circular pattern
**low** [ˈloʊ]: not high
   **lo:** *interjection*
**lowed** [ˈloʊd]: mooed
   **load:** cargo
   **lode:** mineral vein
**lox** [ˈlɔks]: smoked salmon
   **lochs:** lakes
   **locks:** boat elevators, security devices, strands of hair
**lumbar** [ˈlʌmbɚ]: lower back
   **lumber:** milled wood
**lumber** [ˈlʌmbɚ]: milled wood
   **lumbar:** lower back
**lune** [ˈlun]: crescent shape
   **loon:** water fowl
**lurid** [ˈlurɪd]: pale/glowing

**lute** [ˈlut]: stringed instrument
   **loot:** booty
**lye** [ˈlaɪ]: caustic substance
   **lie:** untruth
**lynx** [ˈlɪŋks]: wild cat
   **links:** connections
**lyre** [ˈlaɪɚ]: harp
   **liar:** one who lies

# M

made ['meɪd]: created
　maid: young woman,
　servant
maid ['meɪd]: young woman,
　servant
　made: created
mail ['meɪl]: postal service
　male: masculine
main ['meɪn]: primary
　mane: hair
maize ['meɪz]: corn
　Mays: months of May
　maze: labyrinth
male ['meɪl]: masculine
　mail: postal service
mall ['mɔl]: sheltered walk
　maul: sledgehammer,
　to wound with claws
　moll: gangster's girlfriend
mane ['meɪn]: hair
　main: primary
manner ['mænɚ]: method
　manor: mansion
manor ['mænɚ]: mansion
　manner: method

mantel ['mæntəl]:
　shelf on fireplace
　mantle: cloak, blanket,
　covering
mantle ['mæntəl]: cloak,
　blanket, covering
　mantel: shelf on fireplace
marc ['mark]: coarse brandy
　mark: sign
　marque: brand, license
mark ['mark]: sign
　marc: coarse brandy
　marque: brand, license
marque ['mark]: brand, license
　marc: coarse brandy
　mark: sign
marry ['mɛrɪ]: to wed
　merry: happy
marshal ['marʃəl]:
　high-ranking officer,
　gather together
　martial: military
martial ['marʃəl]: military
　marshal: high-ranking
　officer, gather together
mask ['mæsk]: facial disguise
　masque: amateur dramatics

masque ['mæsk]: amateur
dramatics
mask: facial disguise
massed ['mæst]: assembled
mast: upright pole
mast ['mæst]: upright pole
massed: assembled
maul ['mɔl]: sledgehammer,
to wound with claws
mall: sheltered walk
moll: gangster's girlfriend
Mays ['meɪz]: months of May
maize: corn
maze: labyrinth
maze ['meɪz]: labyrinth
maize: corn
Mays: months of May
mean ['min]:
average/excellent
mien: manner
mean ['min]: meaning, cruel,
average
mien: manner
meat ['mit]: flesh
meet: gather together
mete: to dispense,
boundary

meet ['mit]: gather together
meat: flesh
mete: to dispense, boundary
men's ['mɛnz]: of men
mens: guilty mind
mens ['mɛnz]: guilty mind
men's: of men
merry ['mɛrɪ]: happy
marry: to wed
mete ['mit]: to dispense,
boundary
meat: flesh
meet: gather together
mewl ['mjul]: to whimper
mule: offspring of horse
and donkey
mews ['mjuz]: stables
muse: creative inspiration
mien ['min]: manner
mean: average/excellent
mean: meaning, cruel,
average
might ['maɪt]: power
mite: tiny insect, small
amount, a little
mind ['maɪnd]: brain, to care
mined: excavated
mined ['maɪnd]: excavated
mind: brain, to care

miner [ˈmaɪnɚ]: one who
mines

minor: small child

minks [ˈmɪŋks]: stoats

minx: vixen

minor [ˈmaɪnɚ]: small child

miner: one who mines

minute: [ˈmɪnɪt] *noun*,
[maɪnjˈut] *adj.*

minx [ˈmɪŋks]: vixen

minks: stoats

missed [ˈmɪst]: skipped,
flew past

mist: fog

mist [ˈmɪst]: fog

missed: skipped, flew past

mite [ˈmaɪt]: tiny insect,
small amount, a little

might: power

moan [ˈmoʊn]: groan

mown: cut down

moat [ˈmoʊt]: ditch

mote: tiny piece

mode [ˈmoʊd]: manner, state

mowed: cut down

model [ˈmɔdəl]:
genuine/replica

moderate: [ˈmɔdɚeɪt] *verb*,
[ˈmɔdɚət] *noun*

moire [məˈreɪ]: optical illusion

moray: eel

moll [ˈmɔl]: gangster's
girlfriend

mall: sheltered walk

maul: sledgehammer,
to wound with claws

mood [ˈmud]: emotional state

mooed: lowed (of cow)

mooed [ˈmud]: lowed (of cow)

mood: emotional state

moor [ˈmɔr]: coastal swamp, to
anchor

Moor: North African
Moslem

more: in addition

Moor [ˈmɔr]: North African
Moslem

moor: coastal swamp,
to anchor

more: in addition

moose [ˈmus]: elk

mousse: dessert, hair
styling foam

moot [ˈmut]:
debatable/irrelevant

moray [məˈreɪ]: eel

moire: optical illusion

**more** [ˈmɔr]: in addition
  **moor:** coastal swamp,
  to anchor
  **Moor:** North African
  Moslem
**morn** [ˈmɔrn]: morning
  **mourn:** to grieve
**morning** [ˈmɔrnɪŋ]:
  start of day
  **mourning:** grieving
**mote** [ˈmoʊt]: tiny piece
  **moat:** ditch
**mourn** [ˈmɔrn]: to grieve
  **morn:** morning
**mourning** [ˈmɔrnɪŋ]:
  grieving
  **morning:** start of day
**mousse** [ˈmus]: dessert, hair
  styling foam
  **moose:** elk
**mouth:** [ˈmaʊθ] *noun*,
  [ˈmaʊð] *verb*
**mowed** [ˈmoʊd]: cut down
  **mode:** manner, state
**mown** [ˈmoʊn]: cut down
  **moan:** groan
**mule** [ˈmjul]: offspring of horse
  and donkey
  **mewl:** to whimper

**muse** [ˈmjuz]:
  creative inspiration
  **mews:** stables
**mustard** [ˈmʌstɚd]:
  spicy vegetable seed
  **mustered:** assembled for
  roll call
**mustered** [ˈmʌstɚd]:
  assembled for roll call
  **mustard:** spicy vegetable
  seed

# N

nap [ˈnæp]: short sleep
   knap: break with
   a hammer, crest of a hill
natty [ˈnætɪ]:
   fashionable/bedraggled
naught [ˈnɔt]: nothing
   knot: fastening
   nought: zero
nay [ˈneɪ]: no
   neigh: horse's cry
neap [ˈnip]: lowest tide
   neep: turnip
nearby: [ˈnɪɚˌbaɪ] *adj.*,
   [nɪɚˈbaɪ] adv.
need [ˈnid]: require
   knead: work dough
neep [ˈnip]: turnip
   neap: lowest tide
neigh [ˈneɪ]: horse's cry
   nay: no
new [ˈnju]: not old
   knew: were informed
nice [ˈnaɪs]: pleasant
   gneiss: coarse-grained rock

nickers [ˈnɪkɚz]: those who
   nick
   knickers: women's
   underwear
night [ˈnaɪt]: darkness
   knight: honorary title
nit [ˈnɪt]: louse egg
   knit: to make garments out
   of yarn
nits [ˈnɪts]: louse eggs
   knits: does knitting
no [ˈnoʊ]: negative
   know: to be informed
   Noh: Japanese masked
   drama
nob [ˈnɔb]: rich person
   knob: handle
nock [ˈnɔk]: notch in an arrow
   knock: to rap
nod [ˈnɔd]: head tilt
   gnawed: chewed
noes [ˈnoʊz]: votes against
   knows: is informed
   nose: part of face
Noh [ˈnoʊ]: Japanese masked
   drama
   know: to be informed
   no: negative

**none** [ˈnʌn]: not any
   **nun:** female monk
**nose** [ˈnoʊz]: part of face
   **knows:** is informed
   **noes:** votes against
**nought** [ˈnɔt]: zero
   **knot:** fastening
   **naught:** nothing
**number:** [ˈnʌmbɚ] numeral,
   [ˈnʌmɚ] more numb
**nun** [ˈnʌn]: female monk
   **none:** not any

# O

O's [' oʊz]: more than one O
  owes: is in debt
oar [' ɔr]: paddle
  or: *conjunction*
  ore: mined metal
object: [əb'dʒɛkt] *verb,*
  [' ɔbdʒəkt] *noun*
odd [' ɔd]: strange
  awed: in awe
off [' ɔf]: activated/deactivated
oh [' oʊ]: *interjection*
  haut: high
  owe: be indebted
one [' wʌn]: 1
  won: didn't lose
one's [' wʌnz]: of one
  ones: more than one
ones [' wʌnz]: more than one
  one's: of one
oohs [' uz]: sighs of admiration
  ooze: slime
ooze [' uz]: slime
  oohs: sighs of admiration
or [' ɔr]: *conjunction*
  oar: paddle
  ore: mined metal

oral [' ɔrəl]: of the mouth
  aural: of hearing
ore [' ɔr]: mined metal
  oar: paddle
  or: *conjunction*
ordnance [' ɔrdnəns]:
  bombs and missiles
  ordinance: law, regulation
ordinance [' ɔrdnəns]:
  law, regulation
  ordnance: bombs and
  missiles
original [ə'rɪdʒɪnəl]: old/new
Otto [' ɔtoʊ]: man's name
  auto: aotomobile
ought [' ɔt]: should
  aught: all/nothing
our [' aʊɚ]: belonging to us
  hour: unit of time
ours [' aʊɚz]: belonging to us
  hours: units of time
out [' aʊt]: visible/invisible
out of [' aʊt əv]: outside/inside
outside: [aʊ'tseɪd] adv.,
  [' aʊtsaɪd] *adj.*
overlook [oʊvɚ'lʊk]:
  examine/ignore
overnight: [oʊvɚ'naɪt] adv.,
  [' oʊvɚnaɪt] *adj.*

**oversee** [oʊvɚˈsi]:
control/disregard
**oversight** [ˈoʊvɚsaɪt]:
monitoring/failing
**owe** [ˈoʊ]: be indebted
  **haut:** high
  **oh:** *interjection*
**owes** [ˈoʊz]: is in debt
  **O's:** more than one O

# P

paced ['peɪst]: walked back and forth
  paste: dress jewelry, spreadable mixture
packed ['pækt]: gathered
  pact: agreement
pact ['pækt]: agreement
  packed: gathered
pail ['peɪl]: bucket
  pale: light colored
  pale: restricted area
pain ['peɪn]: suffering
  pane: panel
pair ['pɛɚ]: 2 of something
  pare: cut down
  pear: fruit
pale ['peɪl]: light colored
  pail: bucket
pale ['peɪl]: restricted area
  pail: bucket
pall ['pɔl]: to lose appeal, coffin drapery
  Paul: man's name
  pawl: ratchet lock
pallet ['pælət]: platform, bed
  pallette: selection of colors

pallette ['pælət]: selection of colors
  pallet: platform, bed
pane ['peɪn]: panel
  pain: suffering
pare ['pɛɚ]: cut down
  pair: 2 of something
  pear: fruit
passed ['pæst]: went by
  past: before present
past ['pæst]: before present
  passed: went by
paste ['peɪst]: dress jewelry, spreadable mixture
  paced: walked back and forth
Paul ['pɔl]: man's name
  pall: to lose appeal, coffin drapery
  pawl: ratchet lock
pause ['pɔz]: interruption
  paws: animal's feet
pawl ['pɔl]: ratchet lock
  pall: to lose appeal, coffin drapery
  Paul: man's name
paws ['pɔz]: animal's feet
  pause: interruption

pea ['pi]: green legume
    pee: urinate
peace ['pis]: opposite of war
    piece: part
peak ['pik]: mountaintop
    peek: furtive look
    pique: irritation
peaked: ['pikt] peak,
    ['pikəd] gaunt, pale
peal ['pil]: ringing sound
    peel: fruit skin
pealed ['pild]: rung
    peeled: skinned
pear ['pɛɚ]: fruit
    pair: 2 of something
    pare: cut down
pearl ['pɚl]: gem
    Perl: scripting language
    purl: round stitch
pee ['pi]: urinate
    pea: green legume
peek ['pik]: furtive look
    peak: mountaintop
    pique: irritation
peel ['pil]: fruit skin
    peal: ringing sound
peeled ['pild]: skinned
    pealed: rung

peer ['piɚ]:
    nobility/one's equal
    pier: wharf
pencil ['pɛnsɪl]: writing
    implement
    pensile: hanging down
pensile ['pɛnsɪl]: hanging
    down
    pencil: writing implement
per ['pɚ]: for each
    purr: cat's happy sound
periodic [pərɪ'ɔdɪk]:
    regular/irregular
Perl ['pɚl]: scripting language
    pearl: gem
    purl: round stitch
permit: ['pɚmɪt] noun,
    [pɚ'mɪt] verb
peruse [pə'ruz]:
    pore over/glance at
pharaoh ['fɛroʊ]: Ancient
    Egyptian emperor
    farrow: litter of pigs
phase ['feɪz]: part of
    a sequence
    fays: fairies
    faze: stun

phew [ˈfju]: expression
of relief
  few: not many
phial [ˈfaɪl]: small glass bottle
  file: folder, hand tool
Phil [ˈfɪl]: short for "Philip"
  fill: make full
philter [ˈfɪltɚ]: love potion
  filter: screen
phlox [ˈflɔks]: scented plant
  flocks: groups of birds
pi [ˈpaɪ]: 3.1416...
  pie: baked dish
picnick [ˈpɪknɪk]:
outdoor meal
  pyknic: stocky figure
pie [ˈpaɪ]: baked dish
  pi: 3.1416...
piece [ˈpis]: part
  peace: opposite of war
pieced [ˈpist]: assembled
from pieces
  piste: track of compacted
  snow
pier [ˈpɪɚ]: wharf
  peer: nobility/one's equal
pincher [ˈpɪntʃɚ]:
one who pinches
  pinscher: terrier

pinscher [ˈpɪntʃɚ]: terrier
  pincher: one who pinches
pique [ˈpik]: irritation
  peak: mountaintop
  peek: furtive look
piste [ˈpist]: track of
compacted snow
  pieced: assembled
  from pieces
place [ˈpleɪs]: location
  plaice: flounder
plaice [ˈpleɪs]: flounder
  place: location
plain [ˈpleɪn]: not fancy,
flat ground
  plane: surface
plait [ˈpleɪt]: braid
  plate: dish, flat metal,
  to coat with metal
planar [ˈpleɪnɚ]: flat
  planer: planing tool
plane [ˈpleɪn]: surface,
  plain: not fancy,
  flat ground
planer [ˈpleɪnɚ]: planing tool
  planar: flat
plate [ˈpleɪt]: dish, flat metal,
to coat with metal
  plait: braid

**pleas** [ˈpliz]: requests, admissions of guilt
  **please:** make happy
**please** [ˈpliz]: make happy
  **pleas:** requests, admissions of guilt
**pleural** [ˈplurəl]: relating to lungs
  **plural:** more than one
**plum** [ˈplʌm]: fruit
  **plumb:** vertical, connect with pipe
**plumb** [ˈplʌm]: vertical, connect with pipe
  **plum:** fruit
**plumb** [ˈplʌm]: vertical
  **plum:** fruit
**plural** [ˈplurəl]: more than one
  **pleural:** relating to lungs
**polar** [ˈpoulɚ]: Arctic, Antarctic
  **poler:** one who poles
**Pole** [ˈpoul]: Polish person
  **pole:** stick
  **poll:** opinion survey, vote
**pole** [ˈpoul]: stick
  **Pole:** Polish person
  **poll:** opinion survey, vote

**poled** [ˈpould]: using a pole
  **polled:** covered by opinion survey, lacking horns
**poler** [ˈpoulɚ]: one who poles
  **polar:** Arctic, Antarctic
**poll** [ˈpoul]: opinion survey, vote
  **Pole:** Polish person
  **pole:** stick
**polled** [ˈpould]: covered by opinion survey, lacking horns
  **poled:** using a pole
**pone** [ˈpouni]: dealer's opponent
  **pony:** small horse
**pone:** [ˈpoun] corn, [ˈpouni] gambler's opponent
**pony** [ˈpouni]: small horse
  **pone:** dealer's opponent
**pore** [ˈpɔr]: tiny hole, to study carefully
  **pour:** to dispense liquid, to flow freely
**pour** [ˈpɔr]: to dispense liquid, to flow freely
  **pore:** tiny hole, to study carefully

praise ['preɪz]: approval
  prays: worships
  preys: hunts
pray ['preɪ]: to worship
  prey: to hunt,
  hunted animal
prays ['preɪz]: worships
  praise: approval
  preys: hunts
present: ['prɛzənt] *noun*,
  [prəˈzɛnt] *verb*,
presently ['prɛzəntlɪ]:
  now/soon
prey ['preɪ]: to hunt,
  hunted animal
  pray: to worship
preys ['preɪz]: hunts
  praise: approval
  prays: worships
pride ['praɪd]: high opinion
  of oneself
  pried: opened by prying
pried ['praɪd]: opened
  by prying
  pride: high opinion of
  oneself
pries ['praɪz]: does pry
  prize: award, bounty

prize ['praɪz]: award, bounty
  pries: does pry
produce: ['prɔdjus] *noun*,
  [proʊˈdjus] *verb*
profit ['prɔfət]: net earnings
  prophet: proclaimer of
  God's will
project: [prəˈdʒɛkt] *verb*,
  ['prɔdʒəkt] *noun*
prophet ['prɔfət]: proclaimer
  of God's will
  profit: net earnings
pros ['proʊz]: positives,
  experts
  prose: ordinary language
prose ['proʊz]: ordinary
  language
  pros: positives, experts
psi ['saɪ]: Greek letter
  sigh: sad or tired breath
  xi: Greek letter
public ['pʌblɪk]: social/official
purl ['pɚl]: round stitch
  pearl: gem
  Perl: scripting language
purr ['pɚ]: cat's happy sound
  per: for each
put out ['pʊt ˈaʊt]:
  extinguish/generate

**putting:** [ˈpʊtɪŋ] put,
   [ˈpʌtɪŋ] putt
**pyknic** [ˈpɪknɪk]: stocky figure
   **picnick:** outdoor meal

# Q

**qualify** [ˈkwɔlɪfaɪ]:
restrict/allow

**quantum** [ˈkwɔntʊm]:
huge/tiny

**quarts** [ˈkwɔrts]: more than
one quart
  **quartz:** crystalline rock

**quartz** [ˈkwɔrts]: crystalline
rock
  **quarts:** more than one
  quart

**quay** [ˈki]: wharf
  **cay:** island
  **key:** opens locks

**queue** [ˈkju]: waiting line
  **cue:** signal
  **Kew:** Gardens in London

**quiddity** [ˈkwɪdɪtɪ]:
essense/trifle

**quire** [ˈkwaɪɚ]: 1/20 of a ream
of paper
  **choir:** singers

**quite** [ˈkwaɪt]: somewhat/
entirely

**quoin** [ˈkɔɪn]: cornerstone
  **coin:** money

# R

rack [ˈræk]: shelf, torture
device
 wrack: seaweed, shipwreck
racket [ˈrækət]:
illegal scheme
 racquet: sports equipment
racquet [ˈrækət]: sports
equipment
 racket: illegal scheme
rain [ˈreɪn]: liquid
precipitation
 reign: period of rule
 rein: part of horse's
harness
raise [ˈreɪz]: increase
 rays: more than one ray
 raze: to demolish
completely
rap [ˈræp]: knock, blame
 wrap: covering
rapped [ˈræpt]: knocked
 rapt: spellbound
 wrapped: covered
rapt [ˈræpt]: spellbound
 rapped: knocked
 wrapped: covered

ravel [ˈrævəl]:
entangle/disentangle
ray [ˈreɪ]: shaft of light
 re: musical note D
rays [ˈreɪz]: more than one ray
 raise: increase
 raze: to demolish
completely
raze [ˈreɪz]: to demolish
completely
 raise: increase
 rays: more than one ray
re [ˈreɪ]: musical note D
 ray: shaft of light
re: [ˈri] regarding, [ˈreɪ] de re
read [ˈrɛd]: past tense of
"to read"
 red: color
read [ˈrid]: to read
 rede: advice
 reed: tall marsh grass
read: [ˈrid] present tense,
[ˈrɛd] past tense
reading [ˈridɪŋ]:
gerund of "to read"
 reeding: an architectural
ornament

**reads** [ˈridz]: 3ps of "to read"
  **reeds**: blades of marsh grass
**recall**: [rəˈkɔl] *verb*,
  [ˈrikəl] *noun*
**recede** [rəˈsid]: to move
  backward
  **reseed**: to plant again
**reck** [ˈrɛk]: to pay heed
  **wreck**: ruin, to destroy
**record**: [rəˈkɔrd] *verb*,
  [ˈrɛkəd] *noun*
**red** [ˈrɛd]: color
  **read**: past tense of
  "to read"
**rede** [ˈrid]: advice
  **read**: to read
  **reed**: tall marsh grass
**reed** [ˈrid]: tall marsh grass
  **read**: to read
  **rede**: advice
**reeding** [ˈridɪŋ]:
  an architectural ornament
  **reading**: gerund of
  "to read"
**reeds** [ˈridz]: more than one
  blade of marsh grass
  **reads**: 3ps of "to read"
**reek** [ˈrik]: smell bad
  **wreak**: inflict

**refrain** [rɪˈfreɪn]:
  desist/repeat
**refuse**: [rˈɛfjuz] *noun*,
  [rəfjˈuz] *verb*
**reign** [ˈreɪn]: period of rule
  **rain**: liquid precipitation
  **rein**: part of horse's harness
**rein** [ˈreɪn]: part of horse's
  harness
  **rain**: liquid precipitation
  **reign**: period of rule
**reject**: [ˈridʒəkt] *noun*,
  [rəˈdʒɛkt] *verb*
**rent** [ˈrɛnt]: provide/occupy
**reseed** [rəˈsid]: to plant again
  **recede**: to move backward
**reservation** [rəzəˈveɪʃən]:
  confirmation/uncertainty
**resign**: [rəˈzaɪn] give up,
  [riˈsaɪn] sign again
**resume**: [ˈrɛzjumeɪ] *noun*,
  [rəzjˈum] *verb*
**retch** [ˈrɛtʃ]: vomit
  **wretch**: miserable person
**review** [rəˈvju]: survey
  **revue**: theatrical sketches
**revue** [rəˈvju]: theatrical
  sketches
  **review**: survey

**rheum** ['rum]: mucous
  **room:** compartment
**rheumy** ['rumɪ]: having
  mucous
  **roomie:** roommate
  **roomy:** spacious
**rho** ['roʊ]: Greek letter
  **roe:** fish eggs
  **row:** straight line,
  to pull an oar
**rhumb** ['rʌm]: compass course
  **rum:** liquor made from
  sugar cane
**rhyme** ['raɪm]: verse,
  correpond
  **rime:** frost
**rigger** ['rɪgɚ]: one who rigs
  **rigor:** discipline, symptom
  of high fever
**right** ['raɪt]: opposite of left
  **rite:** ritual
  **wright:** maker
  **write:** to record on paper
**rigor** ['rɪgɚ]: discipline,
  symptom of high fever
  **rigger:** one who rigs
**rime** ['raɪm]: frost
  **rhyme:** verse, correpond

**ring** ['rɪŋ]: circle
  **wring:** twist
**riot** ['raɪət]: violent/funny
**rise** ['raɪz]: stand up, elevation
  **ryes:** grains
**rite** ['raɪt]: ritual
  **right:** opposite of left
  **wright:** maker
  **write:** to record on paper
**road** ['roʊd]: trail
  **rode:** anchor chain or rope,
  travelled
  **rowed:** propelled by oars
**roam** ['roʊm]: to wander
  **Rome:** capital of Italy
**rode** ['roʊd]: anchor chain
  or rope, travelled
  **road:** trail
  **rowed:** propelled by oars
**roe** ['roʊ]: fish eggs
  **rho:** Greek letter
  **row:** straight line,
  to pull an oar
**role** ['roʊl]: part
  **roll:** to rotate, bun, list
**roll** ['roʊl]: to rotate, bun, list
  **role:** part
**Rome** ['roʊm]: capital of Italy
  **roam:** to wander

**rood** ['rud]: cross
  **rude**: impolite
  **rued**: regretted
**room** ['rum]: compartment
  **rheum**: mucous
**roomer** ['rumɚ]: tenant
  **rumor**: gossip
**roomie** ['rumɪ]: roommate
  **rheumy**: having mucous
  **roomy**: spacious
**roomy** ['rumɪ]: spacious
  **rheumy**: having mucous
  **roomie**: roommate
**root** ['rut]: underground part
  of a plant
  **route**: path of travel
**rose** ['rouz]: thorny flowering
  bush
  **rows**: lines
**rot** ['rɔt]: decay
  **wrought**: made
**rote** ['rout]: by memory
  **wrote**: past tense of
  "to write"
**rough** ['rʌf]: coarse
  **ruff**: pleated collar
**rout** ['raut]: to force out,
  disorderly retreat
  **route**: path of travel (US)

**route** ['rut]: path of travel
  **root**: underground part
  of a plant
**route** ['raut]: path
  of travel (US)
  **rout**: to force out,
  disorderly retreat
**roux** ['ru]: sauce
  **rue**: regret
**row** ['rou]: straight line,
  to pull an oar
  **rho**: Greek letter
  **roe**: fish eggs
**row**: ['rau] scandal,
  ['rou] line
**rowed** ['roud]: propelled
  by oars, travelled
  **road**: trail
  **rode**: anchor chain or rope,
  travelled
**rows** ['rouz]: lines
  **rose**: thorny flowering bush
**rude** ['rud]: impolite
  **rood**: cross
  **rued**: regretted
**rue** ['ru]: regret
  **roux**: sauce

**rued** [ˈrud]: regretted
   **rood:** cross
   **rude:** impolite
**ruff** [ˈrʌf]: pleated collar
   **rough:** coarse
**rum** [ˈrʌm]: liquor made
   from sugar cane
   **rhumb:** compass course
**rumor** [ˈrumɚ]: gossip
   **roomer:** tenant
**rye** [ˈraɪ]: grain
   **wry:** mocking, twisted
**ryes** [ˈraɪz]: grains
   **rise:** stand up, elevation

# S

sachet [səˈʃeɪ]: little bag
sashay: strut
sacks [ˈsæks]: bags
sax: saxophone
sail [ˈseɪl]: sheet of canvas
sale: opposite of purchase
sailer [ˈseɪlɚ]: sailboat
sailor: person who sails
sailor [ˈseɪlɚ]: person who sails
sailer: sailboat
sale [ˈseɪl]: opposite of purchase
sail: sheet of canvas
sanction [ˈsæŋkʃən]: approve/penalize
sane [ˈseɪn]: mentally normal
seine: fishing net
saner [ˈseɪnɚ]: more sane
seiner: fisherman
sanguine [ˈsæŋgwɪn]: cheerful/bloodthirsty
sashay [səˈʃeɪ]: strut
sachet: little bag
saver [ˈseɪvɚ]: one who saves
savor: to relish a taste

savor [ˈseɪvɚ]: to relish a taste
saver: one who saves
sawed [ˈsɔd]: past tense of "to saw"
sod: turf
sax [ˈsæks]: saxophone
sacks: bags
scald [ˈskɔld]: burn
skald: Scandinavian bard
scan [ˈskæn]: analyze/skim
scarf [ˈskarf]: garment
scarph: glued joint
scarph [ˈskarf]: glued joint
scarf: garment
scene [ˈsin]: visual location
seen: observed
scent [ˈsɛnt]: smell
cent: 1/100th of a dollar
sent: dispatched
scents [ˈsɛnts]: smells
cents: 1/100ths of a dollar
screen [ˈskrin]: present/conceal
scull [ˈskʌl]: to row
skull: cranium
sea [ˈsi]: ocean
C: letter C
see: to look

seal ['sil]: fasten
    seel: close someone's eyes
        (archaic)
sealing ['silɪŋ]: gluing shut
    ceiling: top of room
seam ['sim]: row of stitches
    seem: to appear
seamen ['simən]: sailors
    semen: seminal fluid
seams ['simz]: rows of stitches
    seems: appears
sear ['sɪɚ]: to scorch
    cere: beak
    seer: prophet
    sere: natural succession
seas ['siz]: oceans
    sees: 3ps of "to see"
    seize: to grab
second: [sɛk'ɔnd] verb,
    ['sɛkɔnd] adj., noun
secrete [sə'krit]:
    produce/hide
see ['si]: to look
    C: letter C
    sea: ocean
seed ['sid]:
    add/remove seeds
    cede: to give

seed ['sid]: germ of a plant
    cede: to give
seeder ['sidɚ]: one who
    plants seeds
    cedar: evergreen tree
seeding ['sidɪŋ]: planting
    ceding: giving
seek ['sik]: to look for
    Sikh: member of religion
seeks ['siks]: looks for
    Sikhs: more than one Sikh
seel ['sil]: close someone's eyes
        (archaic)
    seal: fasten
seem ['sim]: to appear
    seam: row of stitches
seems ['simz]: appears
    seams: rows of stitches
seen ['sin]: observed
    scene: visual location
seer ['sɪɚ]: prophet
    cere: beak
    sear: to scorch
    sere: natural succession
sees ['siz]: 3ps of "to see"
    seas: oceans
    seize: to grab
seine ['seɪn]: fishing net
    sane: mentally normal

seiner [ˈseɪnɚ]: fisherman
saner: more sane
seize [ˈsiz]: to grab
seas: oceans
sees: 3ps of "to see"
sell [ˈsɛl]: to exchange
for money
cell: small room
seller [ˈsɛlɚ]: one who sells
cellar: space under a house
semen [ˈsimən]: seminal fluid
seamen: sailors
sensor [ˈsɛnsɚ]: detector
censer: incense dish
censor: one who impedes
free speech
sent [ˈsɛnt]: dispatched
cent: 1/100th of a dollar
scent: smell
separate: [ˈsɛpɚeɪt] verb,
[ˈsɛpɚət] adj.
sere [ˈsɪɚ]: natural succession
cere: beak
sear: to scorch
seer: prophet
serf [ˈsɚf]: slave peasant
surf: breaking wave
serge [ˈsɚdʒ]: twilled fabric
surge: forceful push

serial [ˈsɪrɪəl]: in series
cereal: grain
series [ˈsɪriz]: sequence
Ceres: Roman goddess
of agriculture
session [ˈsɛʃn]: group meeting
cession: giving up
several [ˈsɛvɚəl]:
single/multiple
sew [ˈsoʊ]: to stitch together
sol: musical note G
sow: to broadcast seeds
sewer [ˈsoʊɚ] one who sews
sower: one who sows
sewer [ˈsuɚ]: sanitation
suer: one who sues
shake [ˈʃeɪk]: vibrate
sheik: Arab prince
shear [ˈʃɪɚ]: to cut
sheer: thin, abrupt turn
shears [ˈʃɪɚz]: cuts
sheers: turns abruptly
sheer [ˈʃɪɚ]: thin, abrupt turn
shear: to cut
sheers [ˈʃɪɚz]: turns abruptly
shears: cuts
sheik [ˈʃeɪk]: Arab prince
shake: vibrate

shelled ['ʃɛld]:
with/without shell

shoe ['ʃu]: footwear

  shoo: to send away

shoes ['ʃuz]: footwear

  shoos: sends away

shoo ['ʃu]: to send away

  shoe: footwear

shoos ['ʃuz]: sends away

  shoes: footwear

shoot ['ʃut]: fire a weapon

  chute: inclined trough,
  parachute

show-stopper ['ʃoʊstɔpɚ]:
admirable/intolerable

sic ['sɪk]: to set upon,
Latin for "thus"

  sick: ill

sick ['sɪk]: ill

  sic: to set upon,
  Latin for "thus"

sics ['sɪks]: sets upon

  six: 6

side ['saɪd]: left or right part

  sighed: breathed
  sorrowfully

sigh ['saɪ]: sad or tired breath

  psi: Greek letter

  xi: Greek letter

sighed ['saɪd]: breathed
sorrowfully

  side: left or right part

sighs ['saɪz]: breathes
sorrowfully

  size: magnitude

sight ['saɪt]: vision

  cite: to reference

  site: location

sighted ['saɪtəd]: seen,
able to see

  cited: referred to

  sited: located

sights ['saɪts]: sees, views

  cites: refers to

  sites: locates

sign ['saɪn]: display,
indication, symbol

  sine: trigonometric function

signet ['sɪgnət]:
authenticating seal

  cygnet: young swan

Sikh ['sik]: member of religion

  seek: to look for

Sikhs ['siks]: more than
one Sikh

  seeks: looks for

**sine** [ˈsaɪn]: trigonometric function

**sign:** display, indication, symbol

**sink** [ˈsɪŋk]: to submerge, drain

**synch:** to synchronize

**Sioux** [ˈsu]: Native American tribe

**sou:** French coin of 5 centimes

**sough:** soft sound

**sue:** to file a lawsuit

**site** [ˈsaɪt]: location

**cite:** to reference

**sight:** vision

**sited** [ˈsaɪtəd]: located

**cited:** referred to

**sighted:** seen, able to see

**sites** [ˈsaɪts]: locates

**cites:** refers to

**sights:** sees, views

**six** [ˈsɪks]: 6

**sics:** sets upon

**size** [ˈsaɪz]: magnitude

**sighs:** breathes sorrowfully

**skald** [ˈskɔld]: Scandinavian bard

**scald:** burn

**skin** [ˈskɪn]: cover/strip

**sore** [ˈsɔr]: hurt, skin ulcer

**soar:** to fly up

**skull** [ˈskʌl]: cranium

**scull:** to row

**slay** [ˈsleɪ]: to kill

**sleigh:** sled

**sleigh** [ˈsleɪ]: sled

**slay:** to kill

**sleight** [ˈslaɪt]: cunning skill

**slight:** not large or strong, insult

**slew** [ˈslu]: past tense of "to slay"

**slough:** bog, sadness

**slue:** to swing around

**slight** [ˈslaɪt]: not large or strong, insult

**sleight:** cunning skill

**sloe** [ˈsloʊ]: blackthorn berries

**slow:** not fast

**slough** [ˈslu]: bog, sadness

**slew:** past tense of "to slay"

**slue:** to swing around

**slough:** [ˈslu] *noun,* [ˈslʌf] *verb*

**slow** [ˈsloʊ]: not fast

**sloe:** blackthorn berries

**slue** [ˈslu]: to swing around
  **slew:** past tense of "to slay"
  **slough:** bog, sadness
**smell** [ˈsmɛl]: sniff/stink
**soar** [ˈsɔr]: to fly up
  **sore:** hurt, skin ulcer
**soared** [ˈsɔrd]: flew up
  **sword:** weapon
**sod** [ˈsɔd]: turf
  **sawed:** past tense
  of "to saw"
**sol** [ˈsoʊ]: musical note G
  **sew:** to stitch together
  **sow:** to broadcast seeds
**sole** [ˈsoʊl]: only
  **soul:** eternal part
**some** [ˈsʌm]: a few
  **sum:** result of addition
**son** [ˈsʌn]: male child
  **sun:** local star
**sonny** [ˈsʌnɪ]: diminutive
  for male child
  **sunny:** lit by the sun
**sore** [ˈsɔr]: hurt
  **skin:** ulcer
  **soar:** to fly up

**sou** [ˈsu]: French coin of
  5 centimes
  **Sioux:** Native
  American tribe
  **sough:** soft sound
  **sue:** to file a lawsuit
**sough** [ˈsu]: soft sound
  **Sioux:** Native
  American tribe
  **sou:** French coin of
  5 centimes
  **sue:** to file a lawsuit
**soul** [ˈsoʊl]: eternal part
  **sole:** only
**sow** [ˈsoʊ]: to broadcast seeds
  **sew:** to stitch together
  **sol:** musical note G
**sower** [ˈsoʊɚ] one who sows
  **sewer:** one who sews
**spade** [ˈspeɪd]: shovel
  **spayed:** sterilized female
  animal
**spayed** [ˈspeɪd]: sterilized
  female animal
  **spade:** shovel
**splice** [ˈsplaɪs]: join/split
**spoor** [ˈspor]: animal trail
  **spore:** single cell
  reproductive body

spore [ˈspɔr]: single cell
reproductive body
spoor: animal trail
staid [ˈsteɪd]: reserved
stayed: remained
stair [ˈstɛɚ]: step on
a stairway
stare: to gaze
stake [ˈsteɪk]: wooden pole,
bet
steak: cut of meat
stanch [ˈstɔntʃ]: stop the flow
staunch: loyal
stare [ˈstɛɚ]: to gaze
stair: step on a stairway
stationary [ˈsteɪʃnɚɪ]:
not moving
stationery: writing paper
stationery [ˈsteɪʃnɚɪ]:
writing paper
stationary: not moving
staunch [ˈstɔntʃ]: loyal
stanch: stop the flow
stayed [ˈsteɪd]: remained
staid: reserved
steak [ˈsteɪk]: cut of meat
stake: wooden pole, bet

steal [ˈstil]: to borrow
without permission
steel: iron alloy
steel [ˈstil]: iron alloy
steal: to borrow without
permission
step [ˈstɛp]: measure,
unit of walk
steppe: level grassland,
prairie
steppe [ˈstɛp]: level grassland,
prairie
step: measure, unit of walk
stile [ˈstaɪl]: narrow passage
style: mode
stoop [ˈstup]: small porch,
to bow down
stoup: drinking cup
storey [ˈstɔrɪ]: floor
story: floor (US), narrative
story [ˈstɔrɪ]: floor (US),
narrative
storey: floor
stoup [ˈstup]: drinking cup
stoop: small porch, to bow
down
straight [ˈstreɪt]: not bent
strait: narrow navigation
channel

strait [ˈstreɪt]: narrow
navigation channel
straight: not bent
strike [ˈstraɪk]: hit/miss
style [ˈstaɪl]: mode
stile: narrow passage
subject: [sʌbˈdʒɛkt] *verb,*
[ˈsʌbdʒəkt] *noun*
succor [ˈsʌkɚ]: relief
sucker: chump,
one who sucks
sucker [ˈsʌkɚ]: chump,
one who sucks
succor: relief
sue [ˈsu]: to file a lawsuit
Sioux: Native
American tribe
sou: French coin of
5 centimes
sough: soft sound
suede [ˈsweɪd]: split leather
swayed: past tense
of "to sway"
suer [ˈsuɚ]: one who sues
sewer: sanitation
suite [ˈswit]: ensemble,
apartment
sweet: sugary

sum [ˈsʌm]: result of addition
some: a few
summary [ˈsʌmɚɪ]:
description
summery: summer-like
summery [ˈsʌmɚɪ]:
summer-like
summary: description
sun [ˈsʌn]: star
son: male child
sundae [ˈsʌndeɪ]: ice cream
with syrup
Sunday: first day of the
week
Sunday [ˈsʌndeɪ]: first day
of the week
sundae: ice cream
with syrup
sunny [ˈsʌnɪ]: lit by the sun
sonny: diminutive
for male child
surf [ˈsɚf]: breaking wave
serf: slave peasant
surge [ˈsɚdʒ]: forceful push
serge: twilled fabric
survey: [sɚˈveɪ] *verb,*
[ˈsɚveɪ] *noun*
suspect: [ˈsʌspəkt] *noun,*
[səˈspɛkt] *verb*

**suspicious** [səˈspɪʃʊs]:
  distrustful/untrustworthy
**swayed** [ˈsweɪd]: past tense
  of "to sway"
  **suede:** split leather
**sweet** [ˈswit]: sugary
  **suite:** ensemble, apartment
**sword** [ˈsɔrd]: weapon
  **soared:** flew up
**synch** [ˈsɪŋk]: to synchronize
  **sink:** to submerge, drain

# T

table [ˈteɪbl]:
advance/withdraw
tach [ˈtæk]: tachometer
  tack: small nail,
  direction of sail
tack [ˈtæk]: small nail,
  direction of sail
  tach: tachometer
tacks [ˈtæks]: small nails,
  directions of sail
  tax: government levy
tail [ˈteɪl]: rearmost part of
  an animal
  tale: narrative
tale [ˈteɪl]: narrative
  tail: rearmost part of
  an animal
tall [ˈtɔl]: high
  tole: painted
  toll: tax or charge
taper [ˈteɪpɚ]: thinner
  at one end, thin candle
  tapir: Malaysian mammal

tapir [ˈteɪpɚ]: Malaysian
  mammal
  taper: thinner at one end,
  thin candle
tare [ˈtɛɚ]: allowance for
  weight of packing materials
  tear: to rip
taught [ˈtɔt]: past tense
  of "to teach"
  taut: stretched tight
taut [ˈtɔt]: stretched tight
  taught: past tense
  of "to teach"
tax [ˈtæks]: government levy
  tacks: small nails,
  directions of sail
tea [ˈti]: herbal infusion
  tee: golfball stand
  ti: musical note B
team [ˈtim]: group of horses
  teem: to swarm
teaming [ˈtimɪŋ]: pairing
  teeming: swarming
tear [ˈtɛɚ]: to rip
  tare: allowance for weight
  of packing materials
tear [ˈtɪɚ]: shed when crying
  tier: horizontal row

111

**tear:** [ˈtɪɚ] cry, [ˈtɛɚ] rip
**teas** [ˈtiz]: more than one tea
**tease:** make fun of
**tees:** more than one
  golfball stand
**tease** [ˈtiz]: make fun of
**teas:** more than one tea
**tees:** more than one
  golfball stand
**tee** [ˈti]: golfball stand
**tea:** herbal infusion
**ti:** musical note B
**teem** [ˈtim]: to swarm
**team:** group of horses
**teeming** [ˈtimɪŋ]: swarming
**teaming:** pairing
**tees** [ˈtiz]: more than one
  golfball stand
**teas:** more than one tea
**tease:** make fun of
**temper** [ˈtɛmpɚ]:
  soften/strengthen
**tenner** [ˈtɛnɚ]: 10-pound note
**tenor:** tendency,
  high-pitched male voice
**tenor** [ˈtɛnɚ]: tendency,
  high-pitched male voice
**tenner:** 10-pound note

**tern** [ˈtɚn]: a shorebird
**terne:** alloy of lead and tin
**turn:** to rotate, change
  of direction
**terne** [ˈtɚn]: alloy of lead
  and tin
**tern:** a shorebird
**turn:** to rotate,
  change of direction
**terrific** [təˈrɪfɪk]:
  wonderful/terrible
**Thai** [ˈtaɪ]: of Thailand
**tie:** a draw, fastening,
  part of formal attire
**their** [ˈðɛɚ]: whose?
**there:** where?
**they're:** who are?
**there** [ˈðɛɚ]: where?
**their:** whose?
**they're:** who are?
**they're** [ˈðɛɚ]: who are?
**their:** whose?
**there:** where?
**threw** [ˈθru]: past tense
  of "to throw"
**through:** from one side to
  the other
**throe** [ˈθroʊ]: spasm of pain
**throw:** to cast

**throes** [ˈθroʊz]: spasms
of pain
  **throws:** 3ps of "to throw"
**throne** [ˈθroʊn]: royal seat
  **thrown:** past participle
  of "to throw"
**through** [ˈθru]: from one side
to the other
  **threw:** past tense
  of "to throw"
**throw** [ˈθroʊ]: to cast
  **throe:** spasm of pain
**throw out** [ˈθroʊ ˈaʊt]:
offer/discard
**thrown** [ˈθroʊn]: past
  participle of "to throw"
  **throne:** royal seat
**throws** [ˈθroʊz]: 3ps of
  "to throw"
  **throes:** spasms of pain
**thyme** [ˈtaɪm]: herb
  **time:** goes from past to
  future
**ti** [ˈti]: musical note B
  **tea:** herbal infusion
  **tee:** golfball stand
**tic** [ˈtɪk]: twitch
  **tick:** click, parasitic insect

**tick** [ˈtɪk]: click,
parasitic insect
  **tic:** twitch
**ticks** [ˈtɪks]: clicks,
parasitic insects
  **tics:** twitches
**tics** [ˈtɪks]: twitches
  **ticks:** clicks,
  parasitic insects
**tide** [ˈtaɪd]: ebb and flow
of ocean water
  **tied:** past tense of "to tie"
**tie** [ˈtaɪ]: a draw, fastening,
  part of formal attire
  **Thai:** of Thailand
**tied** [ˈtaɪd]: past tense
  of "to tie"
  **tide:** ebb and flow
  of ocean water
**tier** [ˈtɪɚ]: horizontal row
  **tear:** shed when crying
**tier** [ˈtaɪɚ]: one who ties
  **tire:** to grow tired,
  rubber wheel cover
**tighten** [ˈtaɪtən]: to make tight
  **titan:** a giant
**til** [ˈtɪl]: until (archaic)
  **till:** until, cash register,
  to cultivate

till [ˈtɪl]: until, cash register, to cultivate

til: until (archaic)

timber [ˈtɪmbɚ]: wood for building

timbre: musical quality of sound

timbre [ˈtɪmbɚ]: musical quality of sound

timber: wood for building

time [ˈtaɪm]: goes from past to future

thyme: herb

tire [ˈtaɪɚ]: to grow tired, rubber wheel cover

tier: one who ties

titan [ˈtaɪtən]: a giant

tighten: to make tight

to [ˈtu]: toward, infinitive

too: also/excessively

two: 2

toad [ˈtoʊd]: amphibian

toed: having toes

towed: pulled along

tocsin [ˈtɔksɪn]: alarm bell or signal

toxin: poison

tocsins [ˈtɔksɪnz]: alarm bells or signals

toxins: poisons

toe [ˈtoʊ]: finger on foot

tow: to pull along

toed [ˈtoʊd]: having toes

toad: amphibian

towed: pulled along

told [ˈtɔld]: past tense of "to tell"

tolled: past tense of "to toll"

tole [ˈtɔl]: painted

tall: high

toll: tax or charge

toll [ˈtɔl]: tax or charge

tall: high

tole: painted

tolled [ˈtɔld]: past tense of "to toll"

told: past tense of "to tell"

ton [ˈtʌn]: 2000 lbs

tonne: 1000 kg

tun: a large cask

tongue [ˈtʌŋ]: muscular organ of the mouth

tung: Chinese tree and oil

tonne [ˈtʌn]: 1000 kg

ton: 2000 lbs

tun: a large cask

**too** [ˈtu]: also/excessively
  **to:** toward, infinitive
  **two:** 2
**tort** [ˈtɔrt]: wrongful act
  or infringement
  **torte:** sweet cake or tart
**torte** [ˈtɔrt]: sweet cake or tart
  **tort:** wrongful act
  or infringement
**tough** [ˈtʌf]: difficult
  **tuff:** stratified
**tow** [ˈtoʊ]: to pull along
  **toe:** finger on foot
**towed** [ˈtoʊd]: pulled along
  **toad:** amphibian
  **toed:** having toes
**toxin** [ˈtɔksɪn]: poison
  **tocsin:** alarm bell or signal
**toxins** [ˈtɔksɪnz]: poisons
  **tocsins:** alarm bells
  or signals
**tracked** [ˈtrækt]: past tense
  of "to track"
  **tract:** a plot of land
**tract** [ˈtrækt]: a plot of land
  **tracked:** past tense
  of "to track"
**transform:** [trənsˈfɔrm] *verb*,
  [ˈtrænsfərm] *noun*

**transparent** [trənsˈpɛrənt]:
  visible/invisible
**transport:** [trənsˈpɔrt] *verb*,
  [ˈtrænspɔrt] *noun*
**tray** [ˈtreɪ]: platter
  **trey:** having 3 of something
**trey** [ˈtreɪ]: having 3
  of something
  **tray:** platter
**trim** [ˈtrɪm]: add/remove
**trip** [ˈtrɪp]: journey, stumble
**troop** [ˈtrup]: company
  of soldiers
  **troupe:** company of actors
**trooper** [ˈtrupɚ]: private
  soldier, state police officer
  **trouper:** staunch colleague
**troopers** [ˈtrupɚz]: private
  soldiers, state police officers
  **troupers:** members of
  a troupe
**troupe** [ˈtrup]: company
  of actors
  **troop:** company of soldiers
**trouper** [ˈtrupɚ]: staunch
  colleague
  **trooper:** private soldier,
  state police officer

**troupers** [ˈtrupəz]: members
of a troupe
    **troopers:** private soldiers,
state police officers
**trussed** [ˈtrʌst]: tied up
    **trust:** faith
**trust** [ˈtrʌst]: faith
    **trussed:** tied up
**tuff** [ˈtʌf]: stratified
    **tough:** difficult
**tun** [ˈtʌn]: a large cask
    **ton:** 2000 lbs
    **tonne:** 1000 kg
**tung** [ˈtʌŋ]: Chinese tree
and oil
    **tongue:** muscular organ
of the mouth
**turn** [ˈtɚn]: to rotate,
change of direction
    **tern:** a shorebird
    **terne:** alloy of lead and tin
**two** [ˈtu]: 2
    **to:** toward, infinitive
    **too:** also/excessively

# U

**unbending** [ə'nbɛndɪŋ]:
  stiff/relaxed
**UNIX** ['junɪks]: operating
  system
  **eunuchs:** castrated men
**urn** ['ɚn]: jar
  **earn:** to make money
**use** ['juz]: to apply
  **ewes:** sheep
  **yews:** trees
**use:** [j'us] *noun*,
  [j'uz] *verb*
**utopian** [ju'toʊpɪən]:
  perfect/unrealistic

# V

vain [ˈveɪn]: proud/futile
   vane: wind indicator
   vein: blood vessel
vale [ˈveɪl]: valley
   veil: head scarf, shroud
vane [ˈveɪn]: wind indicator
   vain: proud/worthless
   vein: blood vessel
variety [vəˈraɪətɪ]:
   distinct type/assortment
vary [ˈvɛrɪ]:
   to differ/to change
   very: extremely
veil [ˈveɪl]: head scarf, shroud
   vale: valley
vein [ˈveɪn]: blood vessel
   vain: proud/worthless
   vane: wind indicator
verses [ˈvə·səs]: lines
   of poetry
   versus: in comparison
   or opposition to
versus [ˈvə·səs]: in
   comparison or opposition to
   verses: lines of poetry

very [ˈvɛrɪ]: extremely
   vary: to differ/to change
vial [ˈvaɪl]: small glass
   container
   vile: despicable
   viol: stringed musical
   instrument
vice [ˈvaɪs]: bad habit
   vise: bench-mounted clamp
vile [ˈvaɪl]: despicable
   vial: small glass container
   viol: stringed musical
   instrument
viol [ˈvaɪl]: stringed musical
   instrument
   vial: small glass container
   vile: despicable
vise [ˈvaɪs]: bench-mounted
   clamp
   vice: bad habit

# W

wade [ˈweɪd]: to walk
through water
weighed: past tense
of "to weigh"
wail [ˈweɪl]: tearful
or frightened cry
wale: ridge, plank, band
whale: large marine
mammal
wails [ˈweɪlz]: tearful
or frightened cries
Wales: country in the west
of Great Britain
wales: ridges, planks, bands
whales: large marine
mammals
wain [ˈweɪn]: wagon
wane: decrease
Wayne: man's name
waist [ˈweɪst]: area between
ribs and hips
waste: trash, scrap,
to use up carelessly
waisted [ˈweɪstəd]: having
a waist
wasted: spent

wait [ˈweɪt]: delay
weight: mass acted upon
by gravity
waive [ˈweɪv]: to give
up rights
wave: sea, oscillation
waiver [ˈweɪvɚ]: contract
for giving up rights
waver: one who is waving
wale [ˈweɪl]: ridge, plank, band
wail: tearful or
frightened cry
whale: large marine
mammal
Wales [ˈweɪlz]: country in the
west of Great Britain
wails: tearful or frightened
cries
wales: ridges, planks, bands
whales: large marine
mammals
wales [ˈweɪlz]: ridges,
planks, bands
wails: tearful or
frightened cries
Wales: country in the west
of Great Britain
whales: large marine
mammals

**walk** [ˈwɔk]: to move on legs, excursion

  **wok:** Chinese cooking pan

**walks** [ˈwɔks]: 3ps of "to walk," excursions

  **woks:** Chinese cooking pans

**wane** [ˈweɪn]: decrease

  **wain:** wagon

  **Wayne:** man's name

**want** [ˈwɔnt]: desire/lack

  **wont:** accustomed

**war** [ˈwɔr]: armed conflict

  **wore:** past tense of "to wear"

**ware** [ˈwɛɚ]: merchandise

  **wear:** attire, endure/succumb

  **where:** here or there

**warehouse:** [ˈwɛɚˌhaʊs] *noun*, [ˈwɛɚˌsaʊz] *verb*

**warn** [ˈwɔrn]: to give warning

  **worn:** past tense of "to wear"

**wary** [ˈwɛrɪ]: careful

  **wherry:** light row boat

**waste** [ˈweɪst]: trash, scrap, to use up carelessly

  **waist:** area between ribs and hips

**wasted** [ˈweɪstəd]: spent

  **waisted:** having a waist

**wave** [ˈweɪv]: sea, oscillation

  **waive:** to give up rights

**waver** [ˈweɪvɚ]: one who is waving

  **waiver:** contract for giving up rights

**wax** [ˈwæks]: substance produced by bees

  **whacks:** strikes, blows

**way** [ˈweɪ]: path

  **weigh:** to measure weight

  **whey:** watery fraction of milk left after forming curds

**Wayne** [ˈweɪn]: man's name

  **wain:** wagon

  **wane:** decrease

**we're** [ˈwɪɚ]: who are?

  **weir:** dam or fence for catching fish

**we've** [ˈwiv]: we have

  **weave:** to make cloth

**weak** [ˈwik]: not strong

  **week:** 7 days

**weal** [ˈwil]: welt, benefit

  **wheel:** round

weald [ˈwild]: rural area
wheeled: having wheels
wield: to hold
wear [ˈwɛɚ]: attire,
endure/succumb
ware: merchandise
where: here or there
weather [ˈwɛðɚ]: state of
the atmosphere,
withstand/deteriorate
wether: castrated ram
whether: or not
weave [ˈwiv]: to make cloth
we've: we have
week [ˈwik]: 7 days
weak: not strong
weigh [ˈweɪ]: to measure
weight
way: path
whey: watery fraction of
milk left after forming curds
weighed [ˈweɪd]: past tense
of "to weigh"
wade: to walk through
water
weight [ˈweɪt]: mass acted
upon by gravity
wait: delay

weir [ˈwɪɚ]: dam or fence
for catching fish
we're: who are?
weld [ˈwɛld]: metal joint
formed by melting
welled: poured forth
welled [ˈwɛld]: poured forth
weld: metal joint formed
by melting
wen [ˈwɛn]: boil or swelling,
runic letter
when: interrogative adverb
or conjunction
were [ˈwɚ]: past tense plural
of "to be"
whir: swishing or
buzzing noise
wet [ˈwɛt]: covered or soaked
with liquid
whet: sharpen blade,
stimulate
wether [ˈwɛðɚ]: castrated ram
weather: state of
the atmosphere,
withstand/deteriorate
whether: or not

**whacks** [ˈwæks]: strikes, blows

**wax:** substance produced by bees

**whale** [ˈweɪl]: large marine mammal

**wail:** tearful or frightened cry

**wale:** ridge, plank, band

**whales** [ˈweɪlz]: large marine mammals

**wails:** tearful or frightened cries

**Wales:** country in the west of Great Britain

**wales:** ridges, planks, bands

**wheel** [ˈwil]: round

**weal:** welt, benefit

**wheeled** [ˈwild]: having wheels

**weald:** rural area

**wield:** to hold

**when** [ˈwɛn]: interrogative adverb or conjunction

**wen:** boil or swelling, runic letter

**where** [ˈwɛɚ]: here or there

**ware:** merchandise

**wear:** attire, endure/succumb

**wherry** [ˈwɛrɪ]: light row boat

**wary:** careful

**whet** [ˈwɛt]: sharpen blade, stimulate

**wet:** covered or soaked with liquid

**whether** [ˈwɛðɚ]: or not

**weather:** state of the atmosphere, withstand/deteriorate

**wether:** castrated ram

**whey** [ˈweɪ]: watery fraction of milk left after forming curds

**way:** path

**weigh:** to measure weight

**Whig** [ˈwɪg]: member of an extinct British/American political party

**wig:** hairpiece

**while** [ˈwaɪl]: during, to waste time

**wile:** cunning

**whiled** [ˈwaɪld]: wasted time

**wild:** untamed

**whine** [ˈwaɪn]: annoying cry or noise

**wine:** fermented grapes

**whined** ['waɪnd]: made unpleasant noise
**wind:** to turn
**wined:** served wine
**whir** ['wɚ]: swishing or buzzing noise
**were:** past tense plural of "to be"
**whirled** ['wɚld]: paste tense of "to whirl"
**world:** the Earth
**whirred** ['wɚd]: made a whizzing or buzzing sound
**word:** a sequence of sounds that has meaning
**whit** ['wɪt]: very small part or amount
**wit:** cleverness, sense of humor
**whither** ['wɪðɚ]: opposite of "whence"
**wither:** to shrivel up
**who's** ['huz]: who is
**whose:** of whom
**whoa** ['woʊ]: command to stop a horse
**woe:** despair
**whole** ['hoʊl]: entire
**hole:** perforation, pit

**wholly** ['hoʊlɪ]: entirely
**holey:** perforated
**holy:** sacred
**whore** ['hɔr]: prostitute
**hoar:** white frost
**whored** ['hɔrd]: prostituted
**hoard:** store or stock of value
**horde:** crowd
**whose** ['huz]: of whom
**who's:** who is
**why** ['waɪ]: for what reason
**wye:** forked support
**Wye:** river between Wales and England
**wicked** ['wɪkəd]: evil/good ['wɪkt]: with a wick
**wield** ['wild]: to hold
**weald:** rural area
**wheeled:** having wheels
**wig** ['wɪg]: hairpiece
**Whig:** member of an extinct British/American political party
**wild** ['waɪld]: untamed
**whiled:** wasted time
**wile** ['waɪl]: cunning
**while:** during, to waste time

wind ['waɪnd]: to turn
whined: made unpleasant
noise
wined: served wine
wind up ['waɪnd 'ʌp]:
end/start
wind: ['wɪnd] moving air,
['waɪnd] to coil
wine ['waɪn]: fermented
grapes
whine: annoying cry or
noise
wined ['waɪnd]: served wine
whined: made unpleasant
noise
wind: to turn
wit ['wɪt]: cleverness, sense of
humor
whit: very small part or
amount
with ['wɪð]: together/against
wither ['wɪðɚ]: to shrivel up
whither: opposite of
"whence"
woe ['woʊ]: despair
whoa: command to stop
a horse

wok ['wɔk]: Chinese cooking
pan
walk: to move on legs,
excursion
woks ['wɔks]: Chinese cooking
pans
walks: 3ps of "to walk,"
excursions
won ['wʌn]: didn't lose
one: 1
wont ['wɔnt]: accustomed
want: desire/lack
word ['wɚd]: a sequence of
sounds that has meaning
whirred: made a whizzing
or buzzing sound
wore ['wɔr]: past tense
of "to wear"
war: armed conflict
world ['wɚld]: the Earth
whirled: paste tense
of "to whirl"
worn ['wɔrn]: past tense
of "to wear"
warn: to give warning
worst ['wɚst]: opposite of best
wurst: sausage
wound: ['wund] injury,
['waʊnd] coiled

**wrack** ['ræk]: seaweed, shipwreck
**rack:** shelf, torture device
**wrap** ['ræp]: covering
**rap:** knock, blame
**wrapped** ['ræpt]: covered
**rapped:** knocked
**rapt:** spellbound
**wreak** ['rik]: inflict
**reek:** smell bad
**wreck** ['rɛk]: ruin, to destroy
**reck:** to pay heed
**wretch** ['rɛtʃ]: miserable person
**retch:** vomit
**wright** ['raɪt]: maker
**right:** opposite of left
**rite:** ritual
**write:** to record on paper
**wring** ['rɪŋ]: twist
**ring:** circle
**write** ['raɪt]: to record on paper
**right:** opposite of left
**rite:** ritual
**wright:** maker
**wrote** ['roʊt]: past tense of "to write"
**rote:** by memory

**wrought** ['rɔt]: made
**rot:** decay
**wry** ['raɪ]: mocking, twisted
**rye:** grain
**wurst** ['wɚst]: sausage
**worst:** opposite of best
**wye** ['waɪ]: forked support
**why:** for what reason
**Wye:** river between Wales and England
**Wye** ['waɪ]: river between Wales and England
**why:** for what reason
**wye:** forked support

# X

**xi** [ˈsaɪ]: Greek letter
    **psi:** Greek letter
    **sigh:** sad or tired breath

# Y

y'all ['jɔl]: you all
  yawl: type of sailboat
yack ['jæk]: make smalltalk
  yak: Tibetan ox
yak ['jæk]: Tibetan ox
  yack: make smalltalk
yawl ['jɔl]: type of sailboat
  y'all: you all
yew ['ju]: tree
  ewe: sheep
  you: 2nd person pronoun
yews ['juz]: trees
  ewes: sheep
  use: to apply
yoke ['joʊk]: part of a harness
  yolk: nucleus of an egg

yokes ['joʊks]: parts
  of harnesses
  yolks: egg nuclei
yolk ['joʊk]: nucleus of an egg
  yoke: part of a harness
yolks ['joʊks]: egg nuclei
  yokes: parts of harnesses
yore ['jɔr]: the past
  your: belonging to you
you ['ju]: 2nd person pronoun
  ewe: sheep
  yew: tree
you'll ['jul]: you will
  yule: Christmas
your ['jɔr]: belonging to you
  yore: the past
yule ['jul]: Christmas
  you'll: you will